NARRATIVE

THE BASICS

Providing an up-to-date and accessible overview of the essentials of narrative theory, *Narrative: The Basics* guides the reader through the major approaches to the study of narrative, using contemporary examples from a wide range of narrative forms to answer key questions, including:

- What is narrative?
- What are the 'universals' of narrative?
- What is the relationship between narrative and ideology?
- Does the reader have a role in narrative?
- Has the digital age brought radically new forms of narrative?

Each chapter introduces key theoretical terms, providing thinking points and suggestions for further study. With an emphasis on applying theory to example studies, it is an ideal introduction to the current study of narrative.

Bronwen Thomas is an Associate Professor in the Faculty of Media and Communication at Bournemouth University, UK.

THE BASICS

NARRATIVE

THE BASICS

Bronwen Thomas

Routledge
Taylor & Francis Group

LONDON AND NEW YORK

First published 2016
by Routledge
2 Park Square, Milton Park, Abingdon, Oxon OX14 4RN

and by Routledge
711 Third Avenue, New York, NY 10017

Routledge is an imprint of the Taylor & Francis Group, an informa business

© 2016 Bronwen Thomas

The right of Bronwen Thomas to be identified as author of this work has been
asserted by her in accordance with sections 77 and 78 of the Copyright, Designs
and Patents Act 1988.

All rights reserved. No part of this book may be reprinted or reproduced or utilised
in any form or by any electronic, mechanical, or other means, now known or
hereafter invented, including photocopying and recording, or in any information
storage or retrieval system, without permission in writing from the publishers.

Trademark notice: Product or corporate names may be trademarks or registered
trademarks, and are used only for identification and explanation without
intent to infringe.

British Library Cataloguing-in-Publication Data
A catalogue record for this book is available from the British Library

Library of Congress Cataloging-in-Publication Data
A catalog record for this title has been requested

ISBN: 978-0-415-83264-9 (hbk)
ISBN: 978-0-415-83265-6 (pbk)
ISBN: 978-1-315-72786-8 (ebk)

Typeset in Bembo and Scala Sans
by Apex CoVantage, LLC

CONTENTS

ACKNOWLEDGEMENTS

My biggest thanks go to the many students who have contributed over the years to discussions on the Narrative Structures unit which I have been teaching since my arrival at Bournemouth University. One of my fondest memories of my time at Bournemouth is of the student who wrote that 'Narrative Structures changed my life' on a course feedback form, and I share that sentiment, having learned a lot from the ways in which my students have applied many of the theories discussed in this book.

The Narrative Research Group at Bournemouth has also been a major source of support and inspiration. I have also been fortunate to have been able to participate in conferences organised by the International Society for the Frontiers of Narrative, and to have published in their journal and in the Frontiers of Narratives series edited by David Herman.

The author and publishers would also like to thank Guardian News & Media Ltd. for permission to quote from the news story in Chapter 4. Thanks also to Arjun Basu and Chindu Sreedharan for permission to reproduce Tweets in Chapter 8.

INTRODUCTION

WHAT IS NARRATIVE?

'Narrative is everywhere that human beings are.'

(Abbott 2008: xv)

'Our sense of reality is increasingly structured by narrative.'

(Fulton 2005: 1)

When the theorist Roland Barthes asserted that narrative 'is simply there, like life itself' (1977: 79), many might have considered his claims a little overblown, as at that time narrative would have been associated more with the imagination, escape and fantasy than with the realities or fundamentals of human life. But Barthes argued that narratives are found all around us, taking many forms and encompassing many modes and media – he used the examples of mime, stained glass windows and comics – demonstrating that narratives may be visual and multimodal as well as being an important part of our oral and written culture. Barthes also showed that narrative isn't a neutral activity, but is political, helping to shape and define the way we respond to the world around us, even how we see and experience that world. Narratives don't just entertain us, therefore, but educate, inform and persuade us, affecting our actions and interactions with one another in all manner of ways.

Narrative theory by no means begins or ends with Barthes. Many studies of narrative open with Aristotle's *Poetics* (384–322 BC), especially his concept of plot as something that is unified and provides a clear beginning, middle and end. With the rise of the novel and the dominance of prose fiction as a storytelling form, many writers reflected on their craft and developed and refined the techniques that we now take for granted. In particular, the figure of the narrator as a companionable guide to the story owes a great deal to the early novels of Fielding and Sterne, and continues into the present with the voice-over in tv and film (see Chapter 3).

Nevertheless, as discussed in Chapter 2, Barthes was one of a group of writers and thinkers in the 1960s and 1970s who transformed the study of narrative and established it as a distinct discipline. Their groundbreaking work initiated what has since become known as the 'narrative turn', not just influencing the humanities, but also the social sciences and, more recently, the sciences, as it has been argued that the human impulse to generate narratives may offer us insights into the very workings of our minds.

Theorists following Barthes have made equally bold claims for the importance of narrative. For example, writing specifically in relation to film, Graeme Turner (2006: 98) acknowledges that while recent movies may focus more on spectacle and special effects than storytelling, it is still the case that 'the world "comes to us" in the shape of stories'. While for some theorists many of the claims made for narrative are so inflated that the term has lost any clarity or precision (e.g. Ryan 2007), as narrative theory engages more and more with other disciplines, its centrality to our understanding of human communication and cognition continues to be asserted.

NARRATIVITY

Narrative theory has long wrestled with the question of what might constitute the essential properties of a narrative, or its narrativity. Most theorists base their definitions on **events**, sequence and causality, as in Porter Abbott's (2008: 13) definition of narrative as 'the representation of an event or series of events', though he goes on to argue that narrative theory has failed to reach consensus on most of the key issues it tries to address. The question of what defines narrative has become particularly important as the discussion has extended to encompass new and emerging media forms, and as the idea of narrative has been used, and some would say stretched, to include nearly every aspect of how we conceptualise our life experiences and everyday reality.

Marie-Laure Ryan (2005) contends that in what she calls the traditionalist view, narrative is conceived of as an 'invariant core of meaning' distinguishing it from all other types of discourse, and allowing it to be transported or carried across time, culture and medium. However, whereas many such theories perceive narrativity to be a quality inherent in a text, others focus more on what we as readers do to activate texts as narrative. For example, Monika Fludernik (1996) argues that we as readers look for ways to understand events as part of a narrative, and so narrativisation is more a reading strategy than a matter of the formal properties of a text. In addition, rather than focusing on plot, Fludernik's definition of narrativity is centred on the notion of experientiality, relying on the presence of some kind of conscious and embodied self with whom we share the emotions and sensations that the narrative evokes.

Marie-Laure Ryan's own definition of narrative conceives of it as a medium-free 'cognitive construct' producing 'the image of a concrete world that evolves in time'. In this view, narrative relies on the reader's 'interest for what comes next, emotional attachment to the characters' (Ryan 2005), something stable and definable, which remains constant across all the different concretisations that a story may take. In this respect, Ryan shares with other theorists the idea of some kind of deep structure or core underlying all the possible varieties of narrative, their surface structure, which helps us to distinguish narrative from non-narrative forms. Nevertheless, Ryan (1992) does allow for different modes of narrativity, including a spectrum from the simple to the complex, in line with other narratologists (e.g. Prince 1982) who have argued for narrativity as a matter of degree. Narrativity may also be differently understood when it comes to visual narratives or music, where the terms visuality, pictoriality and musicality may be used alongside or in opposition to narrativity.

Narrativity or narrativehood may also be understood as an aspect or even a condition of our humanity. For Barthes and his fellow theorists, it is inconceivable that humans could exist without narrative: it is, he claimed 'transhistorical, transcultural', found in every human culture across the globe, and in all the historical and archaeological records we have of human societies. Narrative here is perceived as basic to who we are as human beings, fundamental to explaining how we process time, how memory works and how we come to conceive of our own identities. It is also crucial to how we make sense of the random things and experiences we encounter in our daily lives, helping us to give shape and meaning to them.

In what has been termed the constructivist view of narrative, stories do not just happen, they are made (Bruner 2004 [1987]: 692), and the kinds of stories we have available to us are shaped for us by the particular culture or society we live in. According to this view, narrative imitates life, but life also imitates narrative, meaning that our sense of the world we live in and our idea of ourselves is shaped by this narrativising process.

NARRATIVE AND THE MIND

More recently, it has been argued that narrative forms, especially the novel, build on but in turn help shape and even train our ability to read the minds of others, to empathise with them and imagine ourselves in their shoes. **Cognitive narratology** draws on research from the cognitive sciences and psychology to try to understand how this works and argues that novels and other narrative forms can offer insights into complex psychological states and even pathologies. Stories, it is argued, provide us with scripts that help us to navigate and make sense of experiences that we all share as human beings, almost a kind of 'brain training', but one which encompasses the emotions and our ability to think beyond our immediate and personal needs and desires.

THE END OF NARRATIVE AND NON-NARRATIVES

However, even while the expansion of ideas from narrative theory is proceeding apace and seems to know almost no bounds, critiques of the notion of narrativity as an inescapable aspect of our everyday lives have also been forthcoming. For example, Strawson (2004: 429) takes issue with not just the notion that narrative is an inescapable part of our lives, but that 'Narrativity is crucial to a good life'. Claiming that 'there are good ways to live that are deeply non-Narrative', Strawson contends that the preoccupation with narrativity is potentially dangerous or destructive for those who feel that their lives do not fit the narrative model.

The contention that 'Not everything is narrative' (Schiff 2007) is also made by those who want to argue for the importance of other ways of showing or recording experience or displaying subjectivity, for example, ritual, song, poetry, or dance. Although film and television are now talked about routinely as forms of narrative, as Richardson (2007: 143) reminds us, 'drama has lagged behind' as the distinction between enacting and telling events is maintained. As we shall see in Chapter 8, new technologies may also stretch and challenge our understanding of narrative and its limits, particularly where the real and the fictional become almost indistinguishable, or where the idea of events being made to fit some kind of causal structure seems almost impossible.

Meanwhile, in narratology the term 'unnarratable' (Prince 1987) is used for events that are so incidental or trivial that they do not need to be narrated or events which cannot or should not be narrated because they are taboo (e.g. a character's bathroom visits). Prince (1988) also coined the term the 'disnarrated' to refer to what does not take place, for example, a character's hopes or dreams that never come to fruition or a road not taken by a character.

In the recent past, many commentators claimed that in the wake of the horrific events of 9/11 the appetite for stories, particularly those involving action adventures or fantasy, would be diminished as people would seek out more 'serious' or fact-based ways of coming to terms with what had happened. For a while, it did seem as though blockbuster disaster movies were out of favour, perhaps considered bad taste, but very quickly filmmakers began to create their own narrative accounts of the events of 9/11 (*United 93*, *The Twin Towers*). And, of course, our newspapers and tv screens continuously retold the story of that day through eyewitness accounts, reconstructions and so on.

NARRATIVE ACROSS MEDIA AND CULTURE

In an era of ubiquitous and wearable computing, the idea that we are continually surrounded by stories seems incontestable. Video-games and virtual reality offer us immersive experiences where we can enter into the world of the story and take charge of events, while social networking sites thrive off people sharing stories of their everyday activities or discussing the latest celebrity gossip. The technology may seem new and futuristic, but in many ways these activities only serve to reinforce the idea that human beings will always seek out and want to tell stories, and that they do so in ways which are very familiar, returning to the patterns, structures and character types that storytellers have used since the earliest times. At the same time, as we shall see in Chapter 8, new technologies may provide new affordances for storytelling, allowing readers and users to interact with and even control the narrative or providing us with new ways of understanding narrative, as database or algorithm (Manovich 2001). However, as we try to come to terms with these changes we need to guard against the 'strategic errors' (Ryan 2010: 25) of trying to fit all media into models derived from language-based narratives, ignoring the medium-specific features of film, videogames and so on.

Though early narrative theorists focused almost exclusively on literary texts, they bridged a wide range of disciplines (including anthropology, linguistics, philosophy and literary criticism). It is largely this potential for interdisciplinarity that has made narrative theory so adaptable and amenable to application across a wide range of narrative forms and media. In an age of media **convergence**, where the 'same' story may be told to us on our tv screens, smartphones, in print and online, narrative theory becomes particularly useful and pertinent. At the same time, recent theory has challenged some of the more rigid and formalistic tendencies of the past, with **postclassical narratology** emerging to address the need to embrace a wide range of narrative forms and media, to engage with issues of power and marginalisation and to explore new ways of thinking about narrative. In addition, while narrative theory largely started out as a European and an American affair, today scholars from China and Australasia are helping to redefine the field, and also to challenge the tendency to focus on Anglo-American narratives.

THE STRUCTURE OF THE BOOK

This book shares Barthes's fascination with the workings of narrative, and his belief that understanding the narratives we are surrounded by in daily life is vital if we are to understand and challenge how contemporary societies function, and for whose benefit. So while we will be exploring very basic and seemingly harmless narratives such as fairy tales, popular tv shows or stories told on Twitter, we will find that these narratives shape and define our reality for us in ways that might be limiting, showing us only a version of events, and excluding the experiences of many (e.g. women, the elderly or those from ethnic minorities). Equally, stories may be harnessed for the purposes of persuasion, both in corporate and commercial contexts, but also in politics, influencing how we think of ourselves in relation to specific social structures.

The book is structured in such a way as to introduce you to some of the basic building blocks of narrative – who tells the story, whose point of view we share (Chapter 3), as well as some of the key theories which have helped us to define and understand basic narrative structures (Chapters 1 and 2). This will be supported by reference to contemporary examples from across a wide range of media, helping you to apply these theories and ways of thinking about narrative to the kinds of stories and tales you might enjoy. Later chapters (4 and 5) focus more on how narratives may not only shape but distort events, and the implications for this in terms of politics and power. We will also explore how far narratives are gendered, not only to appeal to male/female audiences, but also to help shape and define what it means to be 'masculine' or 'feminine' in contemporary society. We will then zoom in on specific genres (Chapter 7) to explore in more depth the ways in which crime narratives or real-life stories are structured, and what different kinds of pleasure they may offer us as readers or viewers. The role of the reader and viewer will be explored in depth in Chapter 6, because although traditionally narrative theorists focus on the telling of the story, increasingly audiences and readers participate in helping to construct and retell stories, making it more and more important to take their contributions into account. The huge impact of digital technologies will be explored in Chapter 8, while the conclusion will bring us right up-to-date in terms of some of the latest developments in the field and consider what directions we might see next in terms of the future for narrative and for the study of narrative.

One of the criticisms of narrative theory (and especially Barthes and his contemporaries) is that the terminology used is off-putting and unnecessarily complex. This book will try to avoid jargon where possible, but you will find a glossary of key terms to help you with basic definitions of some of the fundamentals. The best way of getting to grips with narrative theory is to put it into practice, to apply the toolkit you will acquire to the stories and tales you know best and to be prepared to challenge and question those theories where they seem too rigid or inflexible. Where possible, I will illustrate my points with reference to narratives that have a global reach. Where this is not possible, I will either provide generic examples (such as referring more broadly to documentary or first person shooter games) or I will provide some context to help the reader locate and understand the example.

This book does not set out to provide a comprehensive history of the study of narrative, nor does it propose a new model. In particular, this study does not engage with linguistic and social scientific models of narrative. Also, and with apologies to my colleagues, I have not included much by way of discussion of comics and graphic novels Instead, the focus is on demonstrating the wide applicability of the terms and theories developed by narrative theorists, with an emphasis on exploring the specific ways in which narratives continue to enthrall, move and unsettle us in an age when the boundaries between different forms and media, between authors and readers and even between fiction and reality are becoming more and more blurred.

To help you to get started, below you will find some definitions of key terms, plus suggestions for further reading, based on what we have discussed so far. You will also find a Glossary at the end of the book with most terms appearing here marked in bold on first usage.

KEY TERMS

One of the things people find most confusing about studying narrative is that terms that we use to talk about stories and storytelling in everyday conversation may be used differently or with a more specialised meaning.

STORY

Story is used in narrative theory to refer to the chronological sequence of events that underlies the narrative. I often define it as the 'bare bones' of the story, the events that you would include if you wanted to give someone a flavour of what the narrative is about. Narrative theorists talk about story in this way, because it allows us to then begin to analyse the narrative as it is told, to better understand the choices that have been made in that particular telling. So story here is an abstraction, something that has been artificially abstracted from the finished tale.

PLOT

Plot usually refers to the shaping of the story (the chronological sequence of events) into a logical structure which shows the causal connection between those events. This is how we can maximise pleasure and suspense in a narrative (e.g. with clever plot twists), and it is also crucial to how we impose meaning on the story events, by connecting them and showing how they are linked. The novelist E.M. Forster (1963[1927]: 93) famously offered the following as an example of the difference between story and plot. Though many have questioned whether the distinction actually holds up, it's still a useful shorthand way of trying to remember the difference.

Story: 'The king died and then the queen died.'
Plot: 'The king died and then the queen died of grief.'

What plot provides here then is some kind of reasoning or motivation for the events, going a level beyond story in giving shape and meaning to the events recounted.

Narrative theory to date has been dominated by a focus on plot as a means of identifying the underlying structure of a narrative and the events that drive it forwards, and separating this from a focus on the telling of the tale, or narration.

CHARACTER

A character is a participant in the world depicted by the narrative. In many accounts of narrative, characters are secondary to the action, interesting only in so far as they help to drive the action. Sometimes referred to as 'actants', the focus is often on what they do rather than who they are, in terms of personality or psychology. However, this view of character has been challenged by theorists who focus on narrative experientiality (Fludernik 1996) and by cognitive narratologists interested in how the minds of fictional characters are constructed and interpreted by readers.

Characters may also be narrators, recounting events which they took part in either within the storyworld, as **embedded narratives** told to other characters or as the main narrative voice responsible for shaping and creating the storyworld, as is often the case with a **first person narrator** telling of the story of events in which 'I' took part.

NARRATION

Narration refers to the telling of the story. However, much controversy exists in narrative theory as to whether we should refer to a narrating entity or not. Many theorists do personalise the narrator and talk about his or her role in making the choices that bring the story events to life for the reader. The issue becomes especially problematic with screen narratives, where identifying the source of some of these choices may be more complex (is it the screenwriter, the producer, the director, or the editor or the 'auteur'?). Interactive and digital narratives may also problematise how we distinguish between producers and consumers of narrative.

STORYWORLD

The term storyworld can be used interchangeably with fictional world, discourse world and **diegesis** to refer to the real or imaginary environments in which the action of the narrative takes place. In many contemporary franchises, through a process of **worldbuilding** that may involve fans as well as producers and creators, the minute details of these storyworlds may be mapped out across multiple episodes and across different media. The term storyworld may also be used to refer to the mental models that readers and audiences create as they try to make sense of and interpret narratives, imaginatively reconstructing aspects of the context or of the characters' lives that may not be overtly or fully delineated (Herman 2005).

NARRATOLOGY

The term narratology is usually reserved for theories that attempt to provide a systematic model for narrative which can be universally applied (see Chapters 1–3 for examples). Postclassical narratology, which has emerged as a critical and reflexive response to its 'classical' precursor in recent years, moves away from universals and quasi-scientific approaches, to focus more on context and to embrace new perspectives (Herman 1999). Emerging fields would include feminist narratology, cognitive narratology and approaches drawing on linguistics, cultural and media studies and rhetoric. Postclassical narratology engages in dialogue with the three 'posts' of contemporary theory, namely postmodernism, poststructuralism and postcolonialism, for example acknowledging and attempting to redress the Western bias of many of its core concepts. Another of the key shifts in postclassical narratology has been away from purely focusing on the formal properties of texts, to exploring how people respond to stories as stories, inferring and imputing narrative structure based on the skills they have acquired as part of their 'narrative competence' (Herman 1999). At the same time, the object of study has shifted away from the traditional focus on literary texts, to include discussion of media and new media narratives, digitisation and the role of the reader/audience. The following chapters will make reference to many of these new approaches, as well as outlining some of the 'classic' theories to which they respond.

SUGGESTIONS FOR FURTHER READING

The Cambridge Introduction to Narrative by Porter Abbott provides an excellent introduction to some of these foundational issues, especially in Chapters 1 and 2. David Herman's Introduction to *Narratologies* gives a clear and accessible account of the emergence of postclassical narratology, while also offering a good overview of its classical precursors. The *Routledge Encyclopedia of Narrative Theory* is an invaluable resource for anyone interested in narrative theory, providing comprehensive accounts of key terms from leading scholars. For a discussion of narrative in relation to contemporary media, the volume of essays *Narrative and Media*, edited by Helen Fulton is a good introduction, featuring chapters on advertising and magazines, as well as film and television, and engaging with but also critiquing classical narratological terms and models. Nick Lacey's *Narrative and Genre* also provides a very accessible discussion of classical narratological theories with some very contemporary applications from film and television. For studies of narrative that engage with historical and oral traditions, Scholes and Kellogg's *The Nature of Narrative* provides a very readable overview (updated in 2006 with input from James Phelan), while Paul Cobley's more recent study takes a chronological approach, combining discussion of the early roots of narrative with its place in the realist, modernist and postmodernist traditions and considering the impact of new technologies and the role of narrative in the social sciences.

If you are interested in comics and graphic novels, the best place to start is Scott McCloud's *Understanding Comics:* written as a comic it graphically illustrates the concepts of speech bubbles, panels and gutters and focuses on comics as a kind of 'sequential art'. Comic Studies is emerging as a separate discipline, but comics and graphic novels are also increasingly being written about by narratologists (e.g. Kukkonen 2013).

REFERENCES

Abbott, H.P. (2008) (2nd ed.) *The Cambridge Introduction to Narrative.* Cambridge: Cambridge University Press.

Barthes, R. (1977) Introduction to the Structural Analysis of Narratives. In *Image-Music-Text.* Transl. S. Heath. London: Fontana, 79–124.

Bruner, J. (2004[1987]) Life as Narrative. *Social Research*, 71/3, 691–710. Accessed 12/8/15 at http://ewasteschools.pbworks.com/f/Bruner_J_LifeAsNarrative. pdf

Cobley, P. (2014) (2nd ed.) *Narrative.* London: Routledge.

Fludernik, M. (1996) *Towards a 'Natural' Narratology.* London: Routledge.

Forster, E.M. (1963[1927]) *Aspects of the Novel.* Harmondsworth: Penguin.

Fulton, H. (2005) (ed.) *Narrative and Media.* Cambridge: Cambridge University Press.

Herman, D. (1999) (ed.) Introduction. *Narratologies: New Perspectives on Narrative Analysis.* Columbus: Ohio State University Press.

Herman, D. (2005) Storyworlds. In *Routledge Encyclopedia of Narrative Theory*, eds. D. Herman, M. Jahn and M-L. Ryan. London: Routledge, 569.

Herman, D. (2009) *Basic Elements of Narrative.* London: Blackwell.

Kukkonen, K. (2013) *Studying Comics and Graphic Novels.* London: Blackwell.

Manovich, L. (2001) *The Language of New Media.* Cambridge, MA: MIT Press.

McCloud, S. (1993) *Understanding Comics.* New York: Harper Perennial.

Prince, G. (1982) *Narratology: The Form and Functioning of Narrative.* Berlin: Mouton.

Prince, G. (1987) *A Dictionary of Narratology.* Lincoln: University of Nebraska Press.

Prince, G. (1988) The Disnarrated. *Style*, 22, 1–8.

Richardson, B. (2007) Drama and Narrative. In *The Cambridge Companion to Narrative*, ed. D. Herman. Cambridge: Cambridge University Press, 142–55.

Ryan, M-L. (1992) The Modes of Narrativity and Their Visual Metaphors. *Style*, 26, 368–87.

Ryan, M-L. (2005) Narrative and the Split Condition of Digital Textuality. *dichtung-digital*. Accessed 5/3/15 at http://www.dichtung-digital.de/2005/1/Ryan/

Ryan, M-L. (2007) Toward a Definition of Narrative. In *The Cambridge Companion to Narrative*, ed. D. Herman. Cambridge: Cambridge University Press, 22–35.

Ryan, M-L. (2010) Fiction, Cognition and Non-Verbal Media. In *Intermediality and Storytelling*, eds. M. Grishakova and M-L. Ryan. New York: DeGruyter, 8–26.

Schiff, B. (2007) The Promise (and Challenge) of an Innovative Narrative psychology. In *Narrative – State of the Art*. ed. M. Bamberg. Baltimore: Johns Hopkins University Press, 27–36.

Scholes, R., Kellogg, R. and Phelan, J. (2006) *The Nature of Narrative*. Oxford: Oxford University Press.

Strawson, G. (2004) Against Narrativity. *Ratio*, XVII. Accessed 27/3/14 at http://www.lchc.ucsd.edu/mca/Paper/against_narrativity.pdf

Turner, G. (2006) (4th ed.) *Film as Social Practice*. London: Routledge.

BACK TO BASICS

FOLK TALES AND FAIRY TALES

'Myths, folktales, fairy tales – these are the prototypes of all narrative.'
(Scholes 1974: 60)

Most of us are introduced to narratives very early on in childhood. Stories help children to learn and to memorise information. Psychologists are interested in these stories because they also seem to offer children life lessons, preparing them for adulthood and for the physical and emotional upheavals they will face. In *The Uses of Enchantment* (1991), Bruno Bettelheim drew on the theories of Sigmund Freud to show how many familiar folk narratives, such as Little Red Riding Hood and Hansel and Gretel, explored themes of a very dark and often sexual nature. Historians and cultural theorists are also interested in folk tales and what they tell us about the politics of different societies, for example, how various social groups or individuals may be demonised (e.g. wicked stepmothers) or how poverty and mortality affect family relations (as in Cinderella, Jack in the Beanstalk or Snow White). Literary historians and folklorists often trace back the numerous versions of popular tales in order to explore how these retellings reflect current anxieties and fears. For example, Jack Zipes's (1993) study of Little Red Riding Hood showed how in certain societies the tale has been used to warn girls and young women about the dangers of sexuality.

Narrative theorists are more interested in the underlying structures or grammar of these tales and how they seem to be repeated across cultures and time periods. For example, we can find variations on the tale of Cinderella across a wide range of cultures, but also in contemporary reality tv shows or 'chick flicks' where the girl from the poor background gets to go the ball (or high school prom) and wins over her 'prince'. We can also see contemporary ads drawing on the story of the Ugly Duckling, where a beauty product of some kind offers the promise of transforming the duckling into a beautiful swan. For theorists who are trying to get at the underlying structures of narrative, what is shared by narratives told across the world and throughout history, folk and fairy tales offer a way of getting back to basics, of reducing narrative to its most fundamental elements. For example, Umberto Eco's essay 'Strategies of Lying' (1985) uses a structural analysis of Little Red Riding Hood to examine the strategies used by embattled US President Richard Nixon in a 1973 televised speech, turning himself from the villain created by the press into the hero guilty of imprudence and struck down by misfortune who rises up again as defender of the American way of life.

PROPP'S *MORPHOLOGY OF THE FOLK TALE*

One of the pioneers of this approach to narrative was the Russian formalist Vladimir Propp. In his *Morphology of the Folk Tale* (first published in Russian in 1928), Propp focused on the form rather than the content of the tales he studied, emulating a scientific approach (hence the 'morphology' of the title) by looking at large numbers of Russian folk tales and abstracting from them a single structure that could be identified in any tale of this kind. Although there has been some dispute over the exact number of tales Propp studied (some say 100, others closer to 200) and whether he in fact based his morphology on all, or only some, of these tales, his approach radically changed how we conceive of narrative, and has had a huge influence on narrative theory ever since.

What Propp gave us was a kind of template for narrative that breaks it down into 31 functions. These are the components that make up the main action of the tale, with each function occurring in exactly the same position within the overall sequence. Not all of the functions will be found in every tale, but Propp was insistent that when they do occur they always appear in the same sequence. The functions help us to identify recurring types of events in a narrative and how they contribute to driving the narrative along and to building up momentum and suspense. The focus is not on isolated actions or events, but on the consequences actions have as part of a sequence.

The following is John Fiske's (1987: 136–7) summary of Propp's 31 functions, divided into six sequences or stages.

PREPARATION

1. A member of the family leaves home.
2. A prohibition or rule is imposed on the hero.
3. This prohibition/rule is broken.
4. The villain makes an attempt at reconnaissance.
5. The villain learns something about his victim.
6. The villain tries to deceive the victim to get possession of him or his belongings.
7. The victim unknowingly helps the villain by being deceived or influenced by the villain.

COMPLICATION

8. The villain harms a member of the family.
8a. A member of the family lacks or desires something.
9. This lack or misfortune is made known; the hero is given a request or command, and he goes or is sent on a mission/quest.
10. The seeker (often the hero) plans action against the villain.

TRANSFERENCE

11. The hero leaves home.
12. The hero is tested, attacked, interrogated, and, as a result, receives either a magical agent or a helper.
13. The hero reacts to the actions of the future donor.

14. The hero uses the magical agent.
15. The hero is transferred to the general location of the object of his mission/quest.

STRUGGLE

16. The hero and villain join in direct combat.
17. The hero is branded.
18. The villain is defeated.
19. The initial misfortune or lack is set right.

RETURN

20. The hero returns.
21. The hero is pursued.
22. The hero is rescued from pursuit.
23. The hero arrives home or elsewhere and is not recognized.
24. A false hero makes false claims.
25. A difficult task is set for the hero.
26. The task is accomplished.

RECOGNITION

27. The hero is recognized.
28. The false hero/villain is exposed.
29. The false hero is transformed.
30. The villain is punished.
31. The hero is married and crowned.

Propp formulated four observations based on his extraction and analysis of these recurring functions:

1. Functions of characters serve as stable, constant elements in a tale, independent of how and by whom they are fulfilled. They constitute the fundamental components of a tale.

> 2. The number of functions known to the fairy tale is limited.
> 3. The sequence of functions is always identical.
> 4. All fairy tales are of one type in regard to their structure.
>
> (Propp 2003[1968]: 21–23)

In essence, the morphology sets out the idea of narrative as a quest. At the beginning of the story, the hero may be left alone by his or her parents (Function 1, Absentation) and issued with a warning or an order of some kind (Function 2, Interdiction). For example, Red Riding Hood is warned not to stray from the path, and her inability to follow this instruction leads her into the path of the wolf, who plots an act of villainy against her (beginning with Function 4, Reconnaissance). In this instance, the problem is something new that affects the hero, but Propp also identifies a type of story where the problem or 'lack' has been there for some time. So in many folk tales, the hero is sent off on the quest (is dispatched) or decides to go in order to obtain something for a member of the family or resolve the lack (which is often poverty).

With both kinds of story, leaving home and encountering new challenges is an important aspect of the hero's quest, as he or she is tested (Function 12), and usually ends up in combat with the villain (Function 16). The hero is helped by various individuals and by being given some kind of magical agent (Function 14), for example, Jack's magic beans in Jack in the Beanstalk or the sword Excalibur in the tale of King Arthur. Another element of the tale may involve a chase (Function 21, Pursuit), where the hero adopts a disguise or transforms him or herself into an animal or an object of some kind. The tale could end here, but for some heroes further misfortunes and tests face the hero before finally the villain is defeated (Function 30) and the hero receives his or her reward (Function 31, The hero is married and crowned).

We can see that Propp's morphology features many recognisable character types (most obviously the hero and the villain) that we would expect to find in most narratives. But when Propp talks of character, he is concerned not so much with personality or moral worth (i.e. whether or not the hero is a 'good guy'), but with the role that character plays in the action. So he refers to them as dramatis personae or 'spheres of action' rather than as characters, so that whether or not they are heroes or villains depends not so much on who they are as what they *do*. The same character may in fact perform more than one sphere of action (e.g. the same person could be a dispatcher and a donor), while a narrative may also have multiple villains, donors and even heroes. In applying Propp's theory, therefore, it is important to remember that we can't just randomly assign these roles based on who we like or who we think is the 'star' of the movie or show – we need to look at the actions they perform and how their role fits in with that of the other figures who feature in the narrative. The spheres of action are often represented or listed in the following way:

Hero – described by Propp as the 'axis' of the narrative. The hero may be one of two types. A seeker hero (e.g. someone who sets off in search of a missing person). A victimized hero – a character who is seized or banished and is the direct victim of villainy.

Villain – the character who causes harm or injury to the hero or the hero's family.

Donor (or provider) – the person who gives the hero the magical agent after a series of tests and questions.

Helper – magical helpers who carry out various actions in support of the hero.

Dispatcher – usually a parent or authority figure who sends the hero off on the quest.

False hero – someone who presents a false claim to be the hero.

Princess and her father – not distinguished as such by Propp, but the girl or sought-for-person or thing which is often the goal of the quest and the reward of the hero.

APPLICATIONS OF PROPP'S THEORY

Propp's morphology therefore and categorised a narrative structure that is identifiable not just in folk tales but in contemporary narratives of many kinds, the most obvious being narratives for children and action adventure movies where the hero saves the day. For example, Propp has been applied to the Bond movies, with their very recognisable villains (Goldfinger, Scaramanga) and magical agents (the various gadgets given to Bond by the donor figure, Q). The Bond movies also have an established formula whereby Bond is sent on his mission by the dispatcher M, is pursued by various villains and enters into combat with them, before triumphing and usually ending up in bed with the 'princess' on a luxury yacht or other such symbol of wealth and achievement. Television and movie franchises such as *Doctor Who*, *Star Wars* and *Star Trek* have all been analysed using Propp's morphology, demonstrating how popular this type of narrative structure remains with contemporary audiences and how contemporary media and the folk tale 'serve similar functions for their respective audiences' (Turner 2006: 102).

Graeme Turner (2006:102) analyses the main characters from the original *Star Wars* (1977) using Propp's spheres of action:

The villain	Darth Vader
The donor	Obi-Wan Kenobi
The helper	Han Solo
The princess	Princess Leia
The dispatcher	R2-D2
The hero	Luke Skywalker
The false hero	Darth Vader

Some applications of Propp's morphology rely on interpreting the functions nonliterally. For example, in his analysis of David Fincher's complex and dark thriller *Se7en* (1995), Nick Lacey (2000) argues that the 'family' may be interpreted here as the police community of which the hero is a part. Similarly, 'villainy' may be interpreted not as a person but as a state of affairs preventing the hero from attaining his or her goal; the sought-for person may be a goal or something that the hero strives for (e.g. fame, popularity), rather than an actual person; and the magical agent need not be an object but a gift (knowledge, information which helps the hero solve the crime).

We can find this structure repeated in perhaps less obvious contexts, for example, lifestyle or reality tv where the hero lacks something (beauty, fame), receives help and a magical agent from various 'experts' and is transformed and symbolically 'crowned') at the end of the show. Videogame narratives such as *Super Mario Brothers* (1985–) and *Tomb Raider* (1996–) may also be analysed in this way (Newman 2004). And of course we don't have to look far to see innumerable ads that offer us a product as a magical agent to transform us and solve all our woes. However, some theorists (e.g. David Bordwell 1988) see this as stretching, even distorting Propp's morphology and argue that it can only work with contemporary narratives if it is applied loosely or incorrectly.

CRITIQUES AND REAPPRAISALS OF PROPP

Propp remains a divisive figure, his work undermined for many by a flawed methodology and a tendency to overstatement. For example, the claim that 'All fairy tales are of one type in regard to their structure' may seem overly reductive, almost an attack on the idea that narrative should be about creativity and innovation. But many of the attacks on Propp are perhaps more about what's been done *with* the morphology since he wrote it, as Propp himself never looked beyond the Russian wonder tale and his very specific focus on its form. So to accuse Propp of not looking at the cultural context of the tales or looking at tales from other cultures may be considered unfair if this is not what he set out to do.

The morphology does undoubtedly present us with a structure that is about success, about striving and overcoming obstacles for material gain, but rightly or wrongly, this is a structure that we find repeated across Hollywood movies, videogames, ads and novels into the present day. Despite being fiercely critical of some of the ways in which Propp's theory has been misapplied, David Bordwell's analysis of Classical Hollywood cinema identifies a dominant mode in which the focus is on 'individual characters as causal agents' (Bordwell and Thompson 2008: 94) and a narrative in which transformative change is often the direct result of the central character's desires and consequent actions. Such narratives also offer a sense of closure, usually leaving the audience feeling that right has prevailed. Thus in the kind of storyworld we find in classic folk tales and mainstream cinema, there is a sense of an underlying morality in which heroism and villainy are equally uncomplicated, defined by the actions of the characters rather than by any psychological, social or economic factors causing them to behave as they do.

In contrast, many contemporary narratives show us villains winning out or make it difficult to tell who is the hero and who is the villain. Both the movies *Fight Club* (1999) and *Face/Off* (1997) in their own way showed heroes and villains as interchangeable, while for one season of a popular US tv show, the 'heroes' of the title showed their villainous sides. In other movies, for example, *Taken* (2008), the hero may be confronted with complex moral choices resulting in his having to carry out illicit or morally dubious acts in the interests of some kind of greater good.

Propp's theory can be tricky to apply to serialised or epic narratives where we often have multiple heroes and villains and where the sheer length of the narrative means that individual roles will change and the relationships between characters will realign. Remember that Propp's theory is concerned with the idea of a single plot, so where narratives present us with complex interweaving storylines, it can be difficult to identify and unpack the different strands. To some extent, it might even be said that Propp's theory is most useful where it does *not* 'fit', as this helps raise questions about why a given narrative departs from the norm. After all, if all we did when we tried to apply Propp's morphology was tick boxes, it would be a dull and fairly meaningless exercise. Contemporary narratives instead play with narrative and generic conventions. For example, 'offbeat' romance *500 Days of Summer* (2009) eschews the traditional happy ending, while the erotic thriller *Wild Things* (1998) even offered audiences a range of alternative endings, initiating a trend in contemporary films where the narrative spills over into the credit sequence.

Partly because of his subject matter and the time he was writing in, Propp's language can seem rather archaic, as interdictions, reconnaissance and counteraction don't perhaps map easily onto contemporary forms. In addition, the morphology often seems to ramble, making it difficult to follow where each function branches out into so many different variations and possibilities. But if you read Propp's morphology in the original, you will find that he does signpost key elements of the theory to help the reader to navigate through the detail. You will also find that he suggests that the morphology can be used to generate new tales, not just to analyse existing ones. While this was by no means his main intention, it does perhaps explain why Propp's morphology is so often quoted by writers and screenwriters in particular, and has led to the emergence of other models and tools for writers based on mythic structures (notably Joseph Campbell's *The Hero with a Thousand Faces* [1973] and Christopher Vogler's *The Writer's Journey* [1998]).

As we shall see in the next chapter, Propp's work directly influenced many of the classic structuralists. For example, A.J. Greimas (1983[1966]) attempted to produce his own narrative grammar, preferring the term 'actants' to Propp's dramatis personae, reducing them to six (Subject, Object, Sender, Receiver, Helper and Opponent) and distinguishing them from the more particularlised 'actors' (i.e. the actual character who appears in the narrative). Structuralists such as Greimas (1983[1966]) and Claude Bremond (1980), followed Propp in searching for a universal grammar, or the deep structure of narrative (its 'langue', see Chapter 2), producing models and diagrammatic representations that nudged closer and closer to something like a scientific formula.

Lately, there has been a resurgence of interest in Propp's work, thanks to the increasing prominence and influence of the emerging field of the digital humanities. Propp's interest and success in quantifying his corpus of folk tales and abstracting from them a morphological structure that can be applied to a wide range of narrative data provides an important model for approaches that attempt to use computers to analyse and explore huge datasets. Today, rather than morphology, we might talk of Propp's theory as providing us with a kind of DNA for narrative (Lendvai et al. 2010), and he has been the inspiration for the evolution of specific digital tools, including Malec's (online, n.d) development of a Proppian Fairy Tale Markup Language, which is used to explore data structures latent in natural language narratives.

ANALYSIS

Many applications of Propp's theory unfortunately stop short at the level of assigning the spheres of action to specific characters. This does have the benefit of avoiding complexity and what can end up being a retelling of the story or a rather unimaginative mapping of the morphology onto the story events. But it is important always to remember that Propp is concerned with action above character, and he certainly isn't interested in the characters as psychological beings. Though this might go against how we learn to study and evaluate contemporary narratives, it is entirely in keeping with his chosen subject matter: as the writer Philip Pullman (cited by Henley 2013) puts it, 'the fairytale isn't in the business of psychological depth, it's in the business of extraordinary event following extraordinary event', and should be celebrated as such. So applications of Propp should primarily focus on plot, with the 'dramatis personae' only really being of interest in so far as they help to put the actions that drive the narrative into motion.

Of course, with some types of narrative we have to work hard to reconstruct a sense of 'plot', perhaps because the story isn't told in linear order or because it relies on a kind of shorthand to stimulate the reader or viewer's imagination. This is the case with advertising, where there may not be any characters for us to identify with or where nothing much seems to be happening. Nevertheless, we can still read an ad as a narrative which follows the familiar quest structure of Propp's morphology, and which has certain fundamental conflicts at its heart.

In *Mythologies* (1957), his study of contemporary French culture (discussed further in Chapter 4), Roland Barthes devoted a whole chapter to the myths perpetuated by ads for 'Soap Powders and Detergents'. This essay showed that it was possible to take ads seriously, to read and analyse them as we would any other cultural text. Barthes's analysis focused on the ways in which ads rely on a system of signs to put forward a particular ideology or view of the world, but the way in which he talked about ads as relying on myth, and presenting the consumer with various dilemmas and moral choices, also suggests that they can be read as enacting just the kind of narrative sequence that Propp outlines in his morphology.

As Barthes identified, many advertisements for cleaning products focus on the 'evil' of dirt, and suggest that the act of eradicating this evil is somehow heroic. The role of hero in such ads is often assigned to the consumer or viewer, whose 'lack' or 'insufficiency' in Propp's terms is the fact that they have a dirty house, clothes etc. This lack may be one that affects the whole 'family', whether that is the traditional nuclear family or a group of young housesharers, and the solution to this lack (the magical agent which is the product in question) is often recommended to the consumer/hero by a kindly neighbour/friend/expert/scientist who acts as a donor or helper figure. Once the magical agent has been used, and the lack is removed, the ad will typically present us with an image of reward, a symbolic crowning, as the consumer/hero receives love and thanks from his or her family members or is simply shown taking pleasure and joy from the cleanliness/whiteness/freshness of the house/clothes once the magical agent has worked its magic.

While contemporary ads for cleaning products may avoid the hard sell of ads from the past, nevertheless, we can see that familiar and recurring patterns are easily identifiable and that these ads in fact share characteristics with stories from across a wide range of media and genres. For example, we can see elements of the disaster movie in ads which dwell on the nature of the 'evil' faced, while the products themselves, and the dramatis personae responsible for using them, are often granted superheroic qualities. While some might say that ads rely on creating a false or exaggerated sense of lack or insufficiency, for example, dull, lifeless hair or a flawed complexion, they often rely on generating a narrative where the consumer takes centre stage and has to do battle to gain the rewards he or she is after.

CONCLUSION

As we have seen in this chapter, even the most seemingly complex of contemporary narratives often share a basic narrative structure with folk tales, myths and fairy tales. Similarly, postclassical narratology's engagement with cognitive science or computational approaches seems to share a great deal with the attempts of early theorists such as Propp to unearth recurring, familiar patterns across narratives and to understand what kinds of basic human impulses the need to tell stories addresses. In many ways, Propp's morphology has stood the test of time far better than those who came after him and who tried to improve on his model. Testament to this is the fact that Propp's name will in all likelihood be amongst the first you will encounter whether you are studying narrative in the media, literature, history or philosophy, while the attempt to bring a scientific approach to the study of storytelling continues to drive even the most cutting-edge and technologically advanced of research.

SUGGESTIONS FOR FURTHER READING

Bettelheim's *The Uses of Enchantment* offers a fascinating insight into the ways in which childhood tales help shape but also respond to our deepest and darkest imaginings. Jack Zipes's studies of familiar childhood tales focuses more on their social and ideological meanings, while Marina Warner's studies often highlight issues of gender.

Propp's *Morphology*, especially the functions and spheres of action, is widely accessible via the internet. Most studies of narrative, and many introductions to film and media studies, will include reference to Propp, though often the analysis is very superficial. Nick Lacey's *Narrative and Genre* is a welcome exception, providing an interesting analysis of David Fincher's complex thriller *Se7en*. John Fiske's *Television Culture* provides a good overview of Propp's theory in relation to television narratives, while Graeme Turner's *Film as Social Practice* applies Propp to contemporary film examples.

REFERENCES

Barthes, R. (1993[1957]) *Mythologies*. Transl. A. Lavers. London: Vintage.

Bettelheim, B. (1991) *The Uses of Enchantment*. Harmondsworth: Penguin.

Bordwell, D. (1988) ApProppriations and ImProbprieties: Problems in the Morphology of Film Narrative. *Cinema Journal*, 27(3), 5–20.

Bordwell, D. and Thompson, K. (2008) (8th ed.) *Film Art*. New York: McGraw-Hill.

Bremond, C. (1980) The Logic of Narrative Possibilities. *New Literary History*, 11, 387–411.

Campbell, J. (1973) (2nd ed.) *The Hero with a Thousand Faces*. Princeton: Princeton University Press.

Eco, U. (1985) Strategies of Lying. In *On Signs*, ed. M. Blonsky. Baltimore: Johns Hopkins University Press, 3–11.

Fiske, J. (1987) *Television Culture*. London: Routledge.

Greimas, A.J. (1983[1966]) *Structural Semantics: An Attempt at a Method*. Transl. D. McDowell, R. Schleifer and A. Velie. Lincoln: University of Nebraska Press.

Henley, J. (2013) Philip Pullman: 'Loosening the chains of the imagination'. *The Guardian*. Accessed 24/3/15 at http://www.theguardian.com/lifeandstyle/2013/aug/23/philip–pullman–dark–materials–children

Lacey, N. (2000) *Narrative and Genre*. Basingstoke: Macmillan.

Lendvai, P., Declerck, T., Darányi, S. and Malec, S. (2010) Propp Revisited: Integration of Linguistic Markup into Structured Content Descriptors of Tales. Paper presented at the Digital Humanities Conference, King's College

London. Accessed 9/8/2013 at http://dh2010.cch.kcl.ac.uk/academic-pro gramme/abstracts/papers/html/ab-753.html

Malec, S.A. Proppian Structural Analysis and XML Modeling. Accessed 9/8/2013 at http://clover.slavic.pitt.edu/sam/propp/theory/propp.html

Newman, J. (2004) *Videogames*. New York: Routledge.

Propp, V. (2003[1968]) *Morphology of the Folk Tale*. Transl. L. Scott. Austin: University of Texas Press.

Scholes, R. (1974) *Structuralism in Literature: An Introduction*. New Haven: Yale University Press.

Turner, G. (2006) (4th ed.) *Film as Social Practice*. London: Routledge.

Vogler, C. (1998) *The Writer's Journey: Mythic Structures for Writers*. Studio City, CA: Michael Wiese Productions.

Warner, M. (1995) *From the Beast to the Blonde: On Fairy Tales and Their Tellers*. London: Vintage.

Zipes, J. (1993) *The Trials and Tribulations of Little Red Riding Hood: Versions of the Tale in Sociocultural Context*. London: Routledge.

2

NARRATIVE STRUCTURES

'We cannot know the world on its own terms, but only through the conceptual and linguistic structures of our culture.'

(Fiske 1990: 115)

This chapter will focus on the contribution of structuralism to our understanding of narrative. The title encapsulates the dual focus of this movement, as it is concerned both with unearthing the underlying structures that may be found in narratives across time, culture and medium and with how narrative actively structures and shapes our view of the world around us.

'CLASSIC' STRUCTURALISM

Structuralism is largely responsible for the fact that the study of narrative has become commonplace in many humanities subjects, as well as in the social sciences. Structuralism gained credibility because it adopts a systematic approach to the study of narrative and builds on established disciplines, notably linguistics and literary criticism. Many of the key writers associated with 'classic structuralism' in the 1960s and 1970s were French and include Roland Barthes, Claude Lévi-Strauss and Gérard Genette. Though their influence wasn't felt further afield perhaps until the 1980s, it marked a sea change, particularly for the way in which literature was taught in universities in the UK and the US. Whereas previously the focus had been on studying literature in periods, barely moving beyond the text and the immediate context of the life and work of the writer, with structuralism the emphasis switched to theories and models and towards reaching out to other disciplines and intellectual traditions, especially Marxism and philosophy. Just as quickly as it became fashionable, however, structuralism soon lost favour, superseded by poststructuralism and the rise of approaches such as feminist, postcolonialist and queer theory which challenged its universalising tendencies and positivism. However, some of the terms and models introduced by the structuralists have proved durable, particularly for analysing narratives across media and for identifying commonalities and continuities between 'old' and 'new' narratives.

Structuralism derived from structural linguistics and the work of Swiss linguist Ferdinand de Saussure, published in the early decades of the twentieth century based on lectures he had delivered. Saussure focused on studying language as a system of signs, showing that the words we use for objects in the world around us are just as arbitrary as those we use to talk about abstract thoughts and emotions. They only carry meaning as part of a system and because we can differentiate between them and other signs in that system (so we understand 'dog' to mean four-legged hairy creature because the linguistic sign for dog is differentiated from the signs we have for 'cat', 'rabbit' and so on). What this opened up was the possibility that different languages not only have different signs for the 'same' thing, but also that they may cut up the world around them differently. For example, if we compare the words different languages have for colours, they don't always align in terms of the colour spectrum. In my own language, Welsh, for example, the word for blue ('glas') might include shades and hues that we would label green or grey in English (Hjelmslev 1969: 53).

The structuralists extended Saussure's theories to the study of culture, approaching the customs and rituals of specific societies (including their myths and stories) as though they were a kind of language. Attempts to produce a grammar of narrative also drew on Saussure and his distinction between 'langue' (language as a system) and 'parole' (language as it is used by speakers). Alongside Propp, perhaps one of the most widely cited of theorists is the Bulgarian structuralist Tzvetan Todorov.

Todorov's (1971: 39) five basic stages of narrative:

1. A state of equilibrium at the outset
2. A disruption of the equilibrium by some action
3. A recognition that there has been a disruption
4. An attempt to repair the disruption
5. A reinstatement of the initial equilibrium

The simplicity of Todorov's model makes it very appealing and easily applicable across media. For example, Turner's (2006) analysis of the films *Scream* (1996), *Alien 3* (1992) and *Jaws* (1975) demonstrates how each film has very early introductions to the disruption of equilibrium followed by long periods of attempted repair before the restoration of order, however precarious this might be ('Just when you thought it was safe to go back into the water . . .').

SIGNS AND MYTHS

Many structuralists borrowed from Propp's terminology, as in Barthes's (1977) structural analysis of the functions of narrative, and followed his lead in focusing on seemingly basic or 'primitive' narratives such as folk tales and **myths**. In particular, Lévi-Strauss and his strand of anthropological structuralism focused on rites, taboos and myths as sign systems which may offer us insights into the very structures of primitive thinking. Following Propp but also critiquing his approach, Lévi-Strauss (1955, 1966) provided his own structural analysis of myths, including the Oedipus myth from classical antiquity (see Figure 1). But unlike Propp, Lévi-Strauss was more concerned with understanding what these myths and tales tell us about human cultures and how the myths generated and shared by those cultures address the anxieties and contradictions that characterise and shape their worldview. In this respect, as with the work of Roland Barthes, Lévi-Strauss's theories opened up the study of narrative in terms of understanding how stories are related to ideology, to systems of belief which define and shape cultures and the people who live in them.

Whereas Propp focused on a sequential (syntagmatic) analysis of narrative, Lévi-Strauss also analysed how signs are chosen on the basis of association (a paradigmatic analysis). Again, this draws on

Cadmos seeks his sister Europa, ravished by Zeus.			
		Cadmos kills the dragon.	
	The Spartoi kill one another.		
			Labdacos (Laios' father) = *lame* (?)
	Oedipus kills his father, Laios.		Laios (Oedipus' father) – *left-sided* (?)
		Oedipus kills the Sphinx.	
			Oedipus= *swollen-foot* (?)
Oedipus marries his mother, Jocasta.			
	Eteolcles kills his brother, Polynices.		
Antigone buries her brother, Polynices, despite prohibition.			

Figure 1 Structural Analysis of the Oedipus Myth

Saussure's theory of language where words are selected from shared semantic fields (words associated with food, clothing etc.) and combine together syntagmatically to form sentences. Extending this to the analysis of contemporary fashion, individual items of clothing and accessories (ripped jeans, safety pins, tartan) when worn in combination would strongly suggest that the individual wearing these items identifies as a punk.

In Lévi-Strauss's analysis the focus is not only on how events drive the narrative forward, but on exploring the connections created by thematic associations or the 'bundles' of relations that exist between elements of the narrative. Such an analysis is often described as operating on a vertical as well as a horizontal plane, as is clear from Lévi-Strauss's (2000[1967]: 76) diagrammatic representation of his analysis of the Oedipus myth. As Lévi-Strauss goes on to explain, this arrangement is designed to distinguish between the *telling* of the myth (which would disregard the columns) and *understanding* the myth, considering the columns as units exhibiting a common feature (the slaying of a monster in column 3). Although this kind of paradigmatic analysis has been criticised as 'speculative' and difficult to replicate (e.g. Dundes 2003[1968]), it purports to get at the 'deep' layer of a narrative and to connect individual tales and myths to specific cultural world views.

BINARY OPPOSITIONS

Drawing on the importance of difference in Saussure's understanding of how language works, Lévi-Strauss argued that human beings divide the world around them into sets of **binary oppositions**, mutually exclusive categories that set light against dark, up against down, clothed against naked and so on.

Lévi-Strauss's theory helped explain why so many narratives turn on some kind of central conflict between opposing forces. He also showed how fundamental oppositions such as those between good and evil, age and youth, life and death are found across cultures, but are made real or concretised in ways which may be specific to that culture. Studies of film and television narratives in particular have drawn on Lévi-Strauss's notion of binary oppositions. For example, Graeme Turner (2006) analyses the traditional western in terms of a fundamental opposition between culture and nature played out across a range of signifying systems where the homesteaders and the Indians are opposed in the following ways:

homesteaders	Indians
white	red
Christian	pagan
domestic	savage
helpless	dangerous
weak	strong
clothed	naked

(Turner 2006:106)

Zombie myths have also been analysed in this way. Found in a number of cultures, they perhaps speak to our human need to explore the boundaries between life and death and our anxieties about the corporeality of the flesh. But in the zombie movies of the 1970s and 1980s, most notably in George Romero's *Night of the Living Dead* (1968), the zombie becomes a symbol of the worst excesses of consumer culture. More recently, in zombie narratives such as *The Returned* (*Les Revenants*, Channel 4, UK 2013) or *In the Flesh* (BBC3, UK, 2013) the figure of the zombie comes to represent all outsiders, particularly those who are excluded because of their sexuality or ethnicity.

Over time, binary oppositions come to seem natural or obvious to us, and it takes a new approach to remind us that the meanings attaching to them are arbitrary. For example, films such as *Unforgiven* (1992) and *Dances with Wolves* (1990) have explored some of the more uncomfortable aspects of the myths of the western genre, particularly questioning the idea that the homesteaders or cowboys represented civilisation and culture or that their influence was beneficial on the environment they appropriated. *District 9* (2009) does a similar thing with the opposition between aliens and humans, drawing powerful historical parallels with the brutality of the apartheid regime and pointing the finger at contemporary forms of racism and xenophobia to question any simplistic identification of humans and the humane. In a more playful fashion, the teen movie *Scream* (1996) pokes fun at the way in which the horror genre always punishes girls who have lost their virginity (playing on the virgin/whore opposition), and also mocks how the opposition between elements of the setting (inside/outside) or atmosphere (light/darkness) can be manipulated to convey certain moral or emotional states (safety/danger; good/evil).

Reality tv routinely relies on setting up oppositions between groups or types of people, for example, the British tv shows *Supersize vs Superskinny* (Channel 4, UK, 2008–) and *Saints and Scroungers* (BBC One, UK, 2009–). Advertisements also routinely rely on setting up seemingly fundamental oppositions (clean/dirty; lifeless/shiny; natural/artificial) where one side is clearly preferred, so that the consumer is almost morally obligated to choose the 'good' or 'correct' option. What the structuralists set out to do was to show us that none of this is natural or inevitable, but is a product of culture and ideology, and it is important that we recognise this and are alert to the ways in which these cultural narratives act upon us.

So while some of the models proposed by structuralists are so complex and abstract that they are rarely applied and, if so, usually only loosely or in part, some of the key terms and concepts continue to be widely circulated, particularly in the fields of media and cultural studies. This may be because these fields have been traditionally sceptical of literary studies and its focus almost exclusively on textual analysis. Structuralism's attempts at systematicity and the focus on culture as a system of signs has meant that **semiotics**, in particular, has become a cornerstone of the study of a wide range of mainstream cultural practices and modes (film, photography, fashion) as well as subcultures and fandoms.

STORY AND DISCOURSE

Alongside structuralism's focus on narrative grammar, David Lodge (1980) identifies a second project concerned with what he calls the 'poetics of fiction'. In this project, the focus is on understanding the role of the narrator and the relationship between the events of the story and how they are recounted.

In the Introduction, the key distinction between story and plot was introduced. Structuralists developed their own terminology for distinguishing between *what* is being told and *how* it is being told, the most widely used being story (in French, histoire) and discourse (discours). In Chatman's account (1978), story refers to what he calls the content plane, discourse to the plane of the narrative's expression. Other variations include the formalists' distinction between fabula and sjuzhet, or story versus text (preferred by Rimmon-Kenan 1983). Though the terminology can be confusing, particularly as was said earlier the specific way in which structuralists understand 'story', the distinction is fundamental to exposing the choices made in telling any story. What the distinction allows us to begin to explore is the way in which the 'same' story can be told differently, depending on aspects such as where the teller begins the tale, how much time he or she spends on the story events and so on.

In *Narrative Discourse* (1980), Gérard Genette developed his highly influential theory of narrative based on his reading of Marcel Proust's complex exploration of time, memory and identity in *Remembrance of Things Past* (*À la Recherche du Temps Perdu*, 1913). However, his theories have been applied to other media, most notably film, but also to television, comic books and new media narratives. Genette focuses on three aspects of narrative where the relations between story and discourse are especially significant, particularly with regards to time. The first concerns the **'order'** of the discourse, and how this may depart from the chronological order of the story. For example, a narrative may begin with the death of a central character before telling the story of his or her life in **flashback** (as happens in Orson Welles's classic movie *Citizen Kane*, 1941). Alternatively, the narrative may look ahead to events in the future by way of a **flashforward**, as in the US tv show (ABC 2009–10) of that name in which everyone on the planet mysteriously blacks out for a few seconds, giving them a momentary insight into their future destinies, which they then have to come to terms with or try to change. Many contemporary tv shows open with 'teasers' looking ahead to a climactic moment or turning point for the characters. For example, in the tv show *Southland* (2009–), episodes usually open with a shootout or violent incident before turning to the events leading up to the incident, usually involving one of the main characters.

How events are ordered in a narrative may be significant in terms of the importance we assign to them and how we connect those events together, so that if events appear out of chronological sequence we tend to search for reasons why. In contemporary culture, the need to capture an audience's attention has led to many experiments with the order of telling: in *Time's Arrow* (1991) by Martin Amis the story of a Nazi war criminal is told backwards, while in Christopher Nolan's *Memento* (2000) story order is disrupted to reflect the mental condition of the protagonist and his problems piecing together his memories and his sense of his own identity. As Porter Abbott (2008) puts it, a story can't go backwards – like all action it can only go forward in time. But the telling of the story can go in any direction the creator chooses, engaging readers and audiences in new ways, as in Amis's novel where the full 'banality of evil' of the Holocaust is powerfully conveyed.

In the second aspect focused on by Genette, it is the **'duration'** of events that is of concern. When adapting novels to film, screen-writers commonly have to either cut out whole events or speed them up (what Genette calls 'summary' or 'ellipsis'). Thus whereas in the book a whole chapter might be dedicated to a charac-ter's first day at work, in the movie this might be just mentioned briefly in conversation or left out altogether. Conversely, with the filmic technique of slow motion, an event that only takes a second in reality, for example, a punch in a brawl, may be stretched out and viewed from different angles. So more time is taken up with the telling of that event, whereas in the example of the first day at work less time is taken to report on something that may have taken hours or years to unfold in reality. Finally, there may be a close correspondence between the time events take in reality and the time devoted to narrating them (what Genette calls 'scene'). The plots of television soap operas, for example, often unfold slowly in time, with a close correspondence between the time of the events on screen and 'real time' for the viewer. Soaps rely much more on dialogue than other narrative genre, and this can help to contribute to the effect of viewers living through events alongside the characters, as well as seeing the 'same' events from different perspectives.

Genette's final category considered the relations between story and discourse in terms of **'frequency'**, looking at how often the narrative tells us about an event that has taken place. Most common is the 'singulative' instance where we are told once what happened once. If we are told 'repetitively' about the same event, this may suggest that it is particularly noteworthy. It could be that the event is retold by different characters (as in the example of the soap opera) or the same character may revisit the same event from his or her past, perhaps in an attempt to gain some answers about a traumatic or mysterious event. In the movie *Groundhog Day* (1993), comic capital is made from the fact that Phil (played by Bill Murray) becomes stuck in a time loop and has to constantly relive the Groundhog Day festivities in a small town, but ends positively as a life-affirming journey for the character. In the futuristic movie *Source Code* (2011), the central character is forced to relive the same eight minutes of a train journey, only to discover that he is at the centre of a scientific experiment which involves altered states of consciousness and parallel realities, ending in the hero being confronted with a complex moral choice.

At the other extreme, a narrator tells us only once about something that happened more than once (what Genette calls an 'iterative' technique). For example, in a coming-of-age drama, we might be told that a girl and a boy met every day after school in a local café over the course of a summer. The emphasis here is on the series of events taken in total and what they might tell us about this episode in the characters' lives, rather than on the individual events and the shifts and changes that may have affected the relationship.

Genette's work on narrative time has been influential across media, proving invaluable for the analysis of postmodern experiments with nonlinearity and metafiction and for the study of flashforwards and flashbacks in film. In his study of time in contemporary television, Paul Booth (2012: 4) draws on the work of Genette to argue for a 'surge' of shows that feature 'temporal displacement', claiming that these aesthetic changes mirror larger cultural changes taking place, especially the experience of time that we have from social media and online environments. In particular, Booth notes an increase in the use of flashforwards, flashbacks, time travel and changes in the protagonist's memory, and claims that here temporal displacement 'gets the audience more involved in the narrative, allowing them to piece together aspects of the plot' and even offering the audience 'the semblance of control over time' (2012: 5).

Genette's theory added flesh to the bones of the story/discourse distinction, and, as we shall see in the next chapter, this enabled him to go on to explore in much more depth who speaks in a narrative (narration) and from that who sees, hears etc. (the focalizer). However, even though the story/discourse distinction is a fundamental cornerstone of narratology, and comparatively straightforward to grasp and apply, it has not been without controversy, nor has it escaped the tendency of narratologists to constantly redefine and rename key concepts. In particular, disputes have arisen over the extent to which 'story' is separate from discourse, an abstraction or something that is purely 'synthetic' (Phelan 1989) and distinct from aspects of the writer's style or the medium in question. For some, the distinction also breaks down with narratives where trying to work out 'what happened' is almost impossible, for example, in postmodern or experimental fiction which disrupts the very notion of a stable or fixed reality.

POSTSTRUCTURALISM

Such critiques underlie the poststructuralist revision of classic structuralism. Ironically, this was initiated by some of the key players in the classic phase of the movement, most notably Roland Barthes. Poststructuralism has had a huge impact on literary theory in particular, but also suffers from some negativity for its often seemingly impenetrable terminology, and for the fact that many of its main exponents seem more interested in their own activity than in telling us anything interesting about the narratives or texts they are allegedly discussing. Stressing the inevitable subjectivity of any interpretation, this can lead to accusations of navel-gazing and to negative comparisons with the facility with which structuralist models appear replicable and relatively straightforward to apply.

In the late 1960s Barthes and other theorists involved with a journal called *Tel Quel* ('As is/As it is') began to question the possibility of a universal narrative structure. They also pulled apart the very notion of a narrative text as a stable, fixed entity, focusing instead on meaning relations between texts, or what became known as **intertextuality**. The concept of intertextuality was theorised by both Barthes and Julia Kristeva, and has become especially influential in the discussion of postmodern and digital narrative forms (see Chapter 8 for more discussion of this). A fundamental shift was that poststructuralists made a virtue of indeterminacy, fluidity and polysemy, in contrast to the classic structuralists' seeming obsession with being systematic and clear-cut in their approach. As part of this reexamination of the fundamentals of narrative, Barthes proposed a whole new terminology: 'scriptor' instead of 'author', to get away from the traditional notion of the God-like omniscient creator, and a focus on the 'pleasures of the text' as something open-ended, requiring active readers, not passive decoders of preexisting meanings (see Chapter 5). Barthes's notorious announcement of the 'death of the author' and his subsequent theorizing of the role of the reader has been highly influential, especially in the context of contemporary new media narratives, where stories may be produced collaboratively, endlessly customised and reworked (see Chapter 8).

Poststructuralism, like structuralism, is concerned with how language shapes our understanding of ourselves and the world around us, but it takes much further the idea that the relationship between language and our reality is arbitrary and full of contradictions and gaps. In the writings of Jacques Derrida, for example, we find a fundamental critique of many of the notions about language that structuralists seem to take for granted. Instead, language is viewed with distrust, meaning as unstable, something which is never present, but always deferred. Derrida is a key figure in the emergence of deconstruction, a strategy for exposing and teasing out the contradictions of the text and the gaps and inconsistencies that are papered over or covered up. In particular, instead of seeking closure the critic engages in provocation and play, demonstrating the sleight of hand and trickery by which texts appear to present us with coherence and stability.

Poststructuralism is also more openly concerned with ideology, for example, in the work of Foucault (1991) on discourses of power or the French feminists in challenging the hegemony of patriarchy (see Chapter 6). Whereas classic structuralism presented the world as something that could be neatly arranged into sets of binary oppositions suggestive of an either/or logic, poststructuralists showed how loaded and unstable these oppositions often are, for example, in Cixous's (1981) analysis of the way in which cultures set male and female in opposition with one another, with the male terms all being positively weighted and the female negatively. The use of binary oppositions to fix and stabilise hierarchical relations also informs much postcolonial theory, particularly when it comes to challenging the opposition between centre and margin, in which the lives and cultures of anyone outside of Western imperial centres are seen as inferior, impure or worse.

Many poststructuralists were influenced by psychoanalysis, particularly the work of Lacan, opening the way for discussions of narrative that embraced the idea of pleasure, desire and sexuality. A connection between text and body is suggested, and language is seen not as something which is exclusively textual, but as something which also links to our physical, corporeal existence and is driven and shaped by desires and instincts that may be quite deeply buried or repressed. In this respect also, poststructuralism has had a big influence on contemporary gender and queer theories, as well as on studies of cybercultures where the whole relationship between the self and the physical body has been problematised (see Chapters 6 and 8).

CONCLUSION

Although both structuralism and poststructuralism have been primarily concerned with language and textuality, and with literary narratives that often self-consciously experiment with language and notions of sense-making, these theories have also been influential in helping us to explore ways of meaning in a wide range of contemporary practices and discourses. In particular, film theory draws heavily on Lacan and psychoanalysis, while the work of Foucault has been particularly influential in understanding how contemporary media discourses constantly try to exert and maintain power and control over their audiences, but also how audiences are frequently complicit in this through policing their own behaviour or that of others.

FOLLOW-UP ACTIVITIES

1. Discuss how a news story or advertisement relies on setting up some fundamental oppositions between individuals or groups of people.
2. Using two news reports on the same story from different sources, rearrange the events from each in chronological order. Applying Genette's categories of order, duration and frequency, examine

how much time the original reports devoted to each event, how often they were mentioned etc. How does this analysis affect your reading of the two stories?

SUGGESTIONS FOR FURTHER READING

Graeme Turner's *Film as Social Practice* demonstrates how binary oppositions and the disruption and restoration of equilibrium underlie so many contemporary film narratives. He also discusses how Lévi-Strauss's approach helps to highlight the culturally specific meanings attaching to contemporary films. Nick Lacey (2000) also draws on Lévi-Strauss and Todorov in his discussion of film and tv narratives, including *NYPD Blue* and *The X Files*, while also considering how news stories often set up fundamental oppositions between East and West, Us and Them.

REFERENCES

Abbott, H.P. (2008) (2nd ed.) *The Cambridge Introduction to Narrative*. Cambridge: Cambridge University Press.

Barthes, R. (1977) Introduction to the Structural Analysis of Narratives. In *Image-Music-Text*. Transl. S. Heath. London: Fontana.

Booth, P. (2012) *Time on TV: Temporal Displacement and Mashup Television*. New York: Peter Lang.

Chatman, S. (1978) *Story and Discourse: Narrative Structure in Fiction and Film*. Ithaca: Cornell University Press.

Cixous, H. (1981) Sorties. In *New French Feminisms*, eds. E. Marks and I. de Courtivron. Brighton: Harvester, 90–9.

Dundes, A. (2003 [1968]) *Introduction to the Second Edition of Morphology of the Folktale* by V. Propp. Austin: University of Texas Press, xi–xvii.

Fiske, J. (1990) (2nd ed.) *Introduction to Communication Studies*. London: Routledge.

Foucault, M. (1991) *Discipline and Punish: The Birth of the Prison*. Trans. A. Sheridan. London: Penguin.

Genette, G. (1980) *Narrative Discourse*. Transl. J. Lewin. Ithaca: Cornell University Press.

Hjelmslev, L. (1969) *Prolegomena to a Theory of Language*. Transl. F.J. Whitfield. Madison: University of Wisconsin Press.

Lacey, N. (2000) *Narrative and Genre*. Basingstoke: Macmillan.

Levi-Strauss, C. (1955) The Structural Study of Myth. *The Journal of American Folklore*, 68/270, 428–44.

Lévi-Strauss, C. (1966) *The Savage Mind*. London: Weidenfeld & Nicolson.

Lévi-Strauss, C. (2000[1967]) The Structural Study of Myth. In *The Narrative Reader*, ed. M. Mcquillan. London: Routledge.

Lodge, D. (1980) Analysis and Interpretation of the Realist Text: A Pluralistic Approach to Ernest Hemingway's 'Cat in the Rain'. *Poetics Today*, 1/4, 5–22.

Phelan, J. (1989) *Reading People, Reading Plot: Character, Progression and the Interpretation of Narrative*. Chicago: University of Chicago Press.

Rimmon-Kenan, S. (1983) *Narrative Fiction: Contemporary Poetics*. London: Methuen.

Todorov, T. (1971) The Two Principles of Narrative. *Diacritics I*, 1, 37–54.

Turner, G. (2006) (4th ed.) *Film as Social Practice*. London: Routledge.

3

NARRATIVE VOICE AND
POINT OF VIEW

'We are all narrators, though we may rarely be aware of it.'

(Abbott 2008: xii)

'It's the way I tell 'em.'

(Frank Carson, Comedian, 1926–2012)

In Chapter 2 we looked at the distinction between story and discourse that is a basic building block of narrative theory. Once we are
able to identify the choices made in representing the story, this leads
the way to beginning to unpack how the story is told, both in terms
of the narrative voice and in terms of the different perspectives on
events that the narrative may offer us. In describing this layering of
narrative, an analogy is often drawn with the rings of an onion or
a tree, as stories are embedded within each other, or we are offered
more and more perspectives on the 'same' events. Theorists also talk
about the story being filtered or slanted through various perspectives, drawing attention to the fact no matter how transparent or
comprehensive the representation may appear it is always inevitably
restricting us to a particular way of seeing or experiencing events.

At the outer level of the onion rings, we have narration, the telling of the story. Often it is easy to identify the teller of a tale as a
specific individual or personage, perhaps a character who is involved

in the action or the omniscient narrator who looks on from a position 'above' the action, knowing all and seeing all that takes place. However, as mentioned in the Introduction, the question of whether or not every narrative has a narrator in this sense has proved quite controversial, as is applying this terminology to art forms such as film where it may be even more difficult to pin down one creative source or to distinguish between showing and telling.

In his influential analysis of narrative structure in fiction and film, Seymour Chatman (1978) proposes the term 'non-narration' for film, where the effect is as of a viewer overhearing events rather than being addressed by an identifiable individual. Chatman goes on to allow that the term 'minimal narration' may be preferable, and proposes that when looking at the teller or 'transmitting source' (146) we need to allow for a spectrum of possibilities based on the narrator's 'audibility' and 'presence'. Elsewhere, Chatman (1990) uses the term the 'cinematic narrator' to refer to the organising principle or agency whose range and influence can encompass a variety of semiotic channels. Following Chatman, Ciccoricco (2014: 51–2) proposes the term 'cybernetic narration' to account for 'the orchestration of semiotic channels in time', responsible for establishing 'meaningful connections between the technological and the literary' in digital fiction.

The term **'unnatural narration'** (Richardson 2006) has been used in recent narrative theory to account for the phenomenon, particularly in postmodern and experimental narratives, whereby the basic premise or scenario of the narration defies logic or the laws of physics in some way. Examples might include stories narrated by animals or by someone who has died or who hasn't yet been born. Some examples may also be found in popular narrative forms, for example, *The Lovely Bones* (2002) which is narrated by the main character after her murder, or *The Book Thief* (2005) which is narrated by the abstract entity of Death.

Even where we can clearly identify a distinct narrative voice or entity, the inner layers of the onion represent the various ways in which other voices and perspectives may be embedded within the outer layers, offering the reader or audience multiple points of view which may conflict and contradict one another. Narratology offers us the vocabulary to begin to unpick these layers and understand the way in which they relate to one another, but this can be a very complex process and may be a matter of individual interpretation.

THE NARRATOR

In a live storytelling situation, the person telling the story is physically present, and his or her personal charisma, demeanour and skills may produce an immediate, affective response from the audience. Walter Ong (1982) has argued that contemporary media such as television offer audiences a kind of 'secondary orality', compensating for the lack of physical proximity and the sharing of a social space through devices such as direct address or the close up. Ong's term has also been applied in the context of new media technologies (e.g. Thomas 2014) and forms of digital storytelling, such as interactive fiction which uses the second person pronoun, present tense and so on to make users feel as though their responses to what is happening actually influences and directs what might happen next (see Chapter 8).

Choosing a narrative voice appropriate to the narrative and to the audience can be crucial. Think, for example, of movies where the voice-over of a character or onlooker on events may reassure, thrill or terrify us to varying degrees. In the field of advertising, choosing the right voice for a product can be crucial, and ads often will be scheduled to coincide with tv shows in which the voice-over actor is featured, creating a seamless link for the viewer between the entertainment they are enjoying and the particular message that the ad wants to convey. The actor Morgan Freeman has become synonymous with the idea of the silky smooth narrator who can seduce us into thinking anything he wants, a phenomenon that has also come in for ironic mockery in ads such as those for 'More Than' insurance in the UK, where it is revealed that the voice we have been listening to is not that of the great actor, but of an impersonator employed by the ad company to trick us into thinking it's him.

Likewise, reality tv shows such as *Big Brother* use voice-over narration to guide the audience and influence how they react to the events being shown. In the UK version, Marcus Bentley's Geordie accent has become part of the show's branding, but has also been relentlessly mocked. With the reality show *Come Dine with Me* (Channel 4, UK, 2005–), which is set around contestants visiting each other's houses to sample each other's cooking, Dave Lamb, who does the voice-over for the show in the UK, has become notorious for his sarcastic commentary. Not content to describe what is happening, Dave Lamb passes comment on every aspect of the contestants and their homes, and has acquired a cult celebrity status of his own as a consequence. In other shows, on-screen presenters may provide narrative interludes connecting 'before' and 'after' or providing their evaluation of the decisions taken by the show's participants. For example, UK lifestyle tv show *Homes Under the Hammer* (BBC 1, 2003–) has two presenters, male and female, both of whom are experts in transforming 'ugly duckling' properties into desirable residences or profitable investments. In addition to their expert commentary, the show uses nondiegetic music as a way of guiding the viewer's responses. In one episode, for example, the tracks 'Living in a Box' and 'I Believe in Miracles' provide an ironic commentary on that week's properties and the prospects for success of the would-be renovators.

When narratives are adapted from one medium to another, particularly from page to screen, the loss of a text's distinctive narrative voice may be felt keenly. From the early novel onwards, the presence of a narrator as an intimate, trusted companion may be so powerfully felt as to make it almost impossible to imagine that fictional world without that familiar voice. It is difficult perhaps to overstate how influential the concept of the narrator has been not just in the development of the novel form, but in its criticism, as it has helped readers to distinguish between the historical real-world author of a novel and the textual entity and narrative stance that shapes events for us in the telling of the tale.

Of course narrators may be **unreliable**, and their lack of knowledge or willful deceit may be important in helping to sustain suspense. Agatha Christie famously played on the reader's tendency to trust the narrative voice in *The Murder of Roger Ackroyd* (1926), while more recently films such as *The Usual Suspects* (1995) or *Shutter Island* (2010) also feature narrators as plausible guides to events but who conceal as much as they reveal to the audience.

Narrators may employ irony, making it difficult for a reader or viewer to be certain as to their position and opinion with regards to the events they depict. We tend to assume, therefore, that where a narrator conceals something or trips up then it must be deliberate.

However, an interesting question arises as to the extent to which narrators may be unknowingly unhelpful or misleading or where they may be seemingly just as surprised as their audience by the way things turn out.

Narratives may also feature more than one narrator. Jean Rhys's riposte to Charlotte Brontë's *Jane Eyre*, *Wide Sargasso Sea* (1966) features the voices of Antoinetta (based on Bertha Mason) and the husband (based on Mr Rochester), with the husband's section of the narrative coming in between the sections narrated by his wife, telling of her childhood in the West Indies and later her life in England. The effect of this is to undermine the husband's attempt to impose his will on events and to show the instability of both characters' memories and emotions. Again, the technique has also been used in film, for example, *American Hustle* (2013), where the intermittent voice-over narration is shared between the central characters, helping to add to the twists and turns of the plot and keep the viewer guessing as to the characters' true motivations.

When we talk of a narrative voice, what we are pointing to is the expressive and interpersonal potential of this technique, as over the course of reading or watching a narrative we tune in to the distinctive rhythms, inflections and idioms of the narration. This can in turn be thrown into sharp relief in novels which foreground the speech of fictional characters, particularly where those characters use accents and dialects that are distinct from those of the narrator. Irvine Welsh's *Trainspotting* (1993) provided a radical challenge to novelistic convention by having his Standard English narrator appear as the 'odd voice out' in a novel dominated by speakers of Scots vernacular.

TYPES OF NARRATION

Genette's (1980) influential typology of narrators takes as its starting point the relationship of the narrator to the fictional world or diegesis. In his terminology, if the narrator is positioned outside of the events of the narrative, he or she is a **heterodiegetic narrator**, while if he or she takes part in the events of the narrative, he or she is **homodiegetic**. Other theorists prefer to refer to narration from inside the storyworld as dramatised or character narration. Genette uses a theatrical metaphor to further argue that the narrator 'cannot be an ordinary walk-on in his narrative; he can be only the star, or else a mere bystander' (245), and uses the term autodiegetic to refer to the narrator as star.

Genette also distinguishes between different types of narration based on the narrator's position relative to the story; that is, whether the narration is subsequent (classic past tense narration); prior (predicting what will happen either in future or present tense; e.g. in a prophetic or futuristic narrative); simultaneous (as in a running commentary) and interpolated/intermittent (between the moments of the action).

In addition, Genette discusses narration in terms of different levels, using spatial imagery to refer to some acts of narration as being higher than others. The 'highest' level is that of **extradiegetic narration**, told from outside/above the action, as in omniscient narration. Next we have **intradiegetic narration** (told from within the storyworld), and at the third level the metadiegetic (where the telling of the story is taken on by one or more of the characters). Once again, the terminology has proved problematic and controversial, with suggested refinements often compounding the confusion and unsettling the relationship between level and person that Genette tries to instill. The concept of **metalepsis** also complicates things, referring as it does to a transgression of levels where, for example, an extradiegetic narrator intrudes into the diegesis or 'breaks the frame' of the narrative, disrupting the boundaries between the world of the story and the narration in ways which are often, but not always, comic.

Particularly with postmodern narratives, the telling of the story may almost become the main focus, involving the reader or audience in a game where the boundaries between what is real and what is fictional are blurred and creating a hall of mirrors effect where what we think we see is endlessly refracted and even distorted. Many contemporary films and tv shows also play games with the audience, to the point where we may lose faith in the authority and objectivity of the narration. For example, films such as *Crash* (2004) and *Babel* (2006) are structured around multiple retellings of the 'same' events, while US tv shows such as *Lost* (2004–10) or *Breaking Bad* (2008–13) use techniques such as flashback and flashforward to make us question what we have been 'told' or what we think we have 'seen' in previous episodes. *True Detective* (US, 2014) employs the technique of intercutting scenes where the two main characters are interrogated by the police with scenes from their past where they are working together to try to solve the brutal murder of a young girl. Gradually it emerges that one of the characters, played by Matthew McConaughey, is being investigated for wrongdoing, and doubts are cast on the version of events offered by the two men and their seeming success in solving the crime.

The figure of the **narratee** is used in a similar fashion to the narrator to unhook an 'element of the narrative situation' from the real reader. In certain narratives, this narratee is a fully fledged character who is part of the storyworld, but even where the narrative appears to be addressed to no one in particular, Genette (1980) argues, it 'always contains below the surface an appeal to the receiver' (260).

NARRATIVE FRAMING AND EMBEDDING

Framing has been used as a metaphor borrowed from visual art to refer to the separation between the fictional and 'real' world, with the term 'breaking the frame' referring to occasions where the boundaries are blurred (Thomas 2011) as in *Slaughterhouse Five* by Kurt Vonnegut, where the author, in the guise of 'an old fart with his memories and his Pall Malls' (1969: 9), interjects to address the reader directly. Framing is also used to describe how narratives may be embedded in a text: reading *Heart of Darkness* (1899) by Joseph Conrad, many refer to Marlow as the narrator, when in fact his version of events is recounted by an unnamed man on a boat with whom the narrative begins and ends. In film, a voice-over may be used as a framing device, bookending the main action and placing the viewer at a remove from events. The framing work of a narrator may be quite unobtrusive as he or she sets the scene then withdraws. However, even if the framing comments appear quite innocuous, they nevertheless shape and inform how we react to the ensuing action.

In addition to the framing work of a narrator, narrative texts may also be framed by paratextual material. In the case of a novel, this might be a preface or an author biography. In the case of a movie, this might be a trailer, posters, or other prepublicity. As discussed in Chapter 8, recent studies have suggested that far from seeing such material as peripheral or incidental to the 'main' narrative, it can instead be seen as contributing significantly to the reader's or viewer's understanding of a text and the pleasure he or she derives from it.

Where multiple embedding of narratives occurs, the metaphors of 'Chinese boxes' or 'Russian dolls' are used to help convey the idea of stories 'nesting' within one another. While the metaphor of the frame implies some sense of fixity or stability, in postmodern works multiple embedding can be quite dizzying, unsettling the reader or viewer and creating some uncertainty about how various accounts might ever be pieced together. When it comes to hypertext or non-linear narratives, it may be that we have to abandon the metaphor of the frame altogether, as every reading may present the reader with a different sense of how the layers of the narrative might relate to one another. For this reason, Marie-Laure Ryan (1990) suggests that that we should replace the metaphor of the frame for that of the stack, derived from the language of computer programming. In this conceptualisation, like plates stacked on top of each other, the movement of one element impacts on the others in a way that is dynamic rather than static or fixed from the outset.

FOCALIZATION

Tucked away in a chapter on 'Mood' in which he discusses the various techniques at the novelist's disposal for representing speech, Genette turns his attention to perspective. Distinguishing between mood and voice, between who sees and who speaks, Genette introduced the term **focalization** as a corrective to what he saw as the confusion between point of view and narration which had characterised theories of narrative to date. Focalization was intended to avoid the visual connotations of point of view, and has become the preferred term in narrative studies, though not without much debate and refinement, much of which is still ongoing. As Seymour Chatman (1978: 151) puts it, point of view remains 'one of the most troublesome of critical terms', partly because we so commonly use the terms 'view' and 'see' metaphorically.

According to Jahn (2005), the concept of focalization owes much to **modernist literature** and its radical break from some of the traditions of the realist novel. In particular, modernist fiction often invites us to question what we think we know, and even what we think we see, by offering us multiple perspectives on events and challenging the idea that reality can be (re)presented to us as something that is transparent. Modernist literature seems to make a virtue out of offering the reader only partial or limited glimpses of events, whether because of the limitations of the focalized characters or because the narrative chooses not to present us with the 'whole story'.

While the narrator is the one who tells the story and 'speaks' in the text, the events of the narrative may be represented from the perspective of other individuals or even groups of individuals from within the storyworld, conveying their sensations, emotions and beliefs in such a fashion that the reader or viewer appears to experience them alongside or through that character. As Murphet (2005: 89) puts it, 'Focalization becomes an issue when we shift into the diegetic world and begin to have our perceptions and thoughts shaped by the characters who attract and direct narrative discourse' (89). This accounts for one of the main characteristics of narrative, perhaps especially literary fiction, as it can create the impression for the reader that we are living the moment with the fictional character, hearing what he or she hears, feeling his or her pain etc. One of the most vivid examples of this comes from William Golding's *Pincher Martin* (1956: 7), which opens with a scene in which a character is drowning:

> When the air had gone with the shriek, water came in to fill its place – burning water, hard in the throat and mouth as stones that hurt. He hutched his body towards the place where air had been but now it was gone and there was nothing but black, choking welter.

The speaker or teller of the tale is not the boy who is drowning, but the language of the passage vividly recreates for the reader the experience, breath by breath, as it were, immersing us in the character's physical and psychological reactions in a highly dramatic opening to the novel. This technique of thrusting the reader or viewer into a situation of danger or threat before gradually revealing the circumstances leading up to the event and providing the experience with some kind of context is one that will also be familiar from films and videogames. For example, in the first person shooter genre, the player enters the action and experiences the storyworld from a perspective very close to the on-screen avatar, as he or she controls the movement of the avatar but is restricted to what he or she can do within the context of the scenario of a particular scene or level of the game.

POINT OF VIEW AND IDEOLOGY

Analysing focalization in a narrative often means examining form and technique in minute detail. Susan Lanser (1981) warns that this can result in a kind of 'pseudoscientfic myopia' (15) and maintains that it is important that narratological approaches focus on questions of ideology that arise from the way in which events or experiences are portrayed. Lanser also argues that we can recognise cultural preferences and patterns in the representations of point of view that we find in a particular period or movement: for example, at the beginning of the twentieth century, and the rise of literary modernism, she claims that there is a distinct preference for indirect or oblique techniques.

Lanser's approach brings into question whether it is ever possible to have an unfiltered or completely objective view of reality. Certainly, representing the perspective of an individual can be highly persuasive, drawing on the emotions and reactions of that individual as he or she is caught up in events. Charities and governmental organisations often rely on shock tactics to help educate or warn people about certain dangers, putting us in the situation of an autistic child as in 'Auti-Sim' (http://www.gamesforchange.org/play/autisim/) or offering us the perspective of a victim of domestic violence seen through Google Glass in the project 'A woman's day #throughglass' (https://www.youtube.com/watch?v=MN4sMISyYgk).

In news stories, the perspective from which events are relayed to us may be significant in terms of how we apportion blame or responsibility. For example, eyewitness accounts from the point of view of a victim of a drone attack may emphasise the widespread devastation caused. However, if the account of the drone pilot or another member of the military is given, perhaps this might present the same attack as a feat of surgical precision. Visually, camera angles help to place us in relation to events in such a way as to influence our response. Many images in the press depicting the Palestinian-Israeli conflict play on David and Goliath imagery, with young Palestinian boys shown throwing stones at Israeli tanks seemingly bearing down on them. However, in many of the same shots, had the camera been positioned behind the tank, the view might be quite different, for example, showing the boy as part of an angry crowd, thus reversing the roles of victims and aggressors.

FOCALIZATION IN VISUAL NARRATIVES

For the purposes of entertainment and sensation, whole movies such as *Gravity* (2013) may rely heavily on recreating a particular physical state for the audience, allowing us to experience seemingly firsthand the dangers and the comic moments that astronauts experience as part of the routine of space travel. This can be powerful stuff, discomfiting at times, but thrilling, especially where the storyteller engages our senses in a new or thought-provoking way. In Spielberg's *Saving Private Ryan* (1998), for example, the sight but particularly the sound of bullets whizzing by takes viewers into the heart of battle in a way which conveys the physical disorientation experienced by soldiers on the ground.

In a novel, we can seemingly enter the mind of a character, and experience the same sensations as that character, as in the example from *Pincher Martin* cited earlier. With visual narratives, the mechanisms for offering us this same kind of 'insider viewpoint' are generally more obtrusive and therefore less immersive. One option is to have a character tell us what he or she is thinking, either in conversation with another character or by means of a voice-over. The 'point-of-view shot' offers us the opportunity to share a character's perceptual field, but it is usually reserved for scenes where these perceptions are disturbed, for example, in a dream sequence or where the character is hallucinating. In the American tv show *True Blood* (HBO, 2008–14), the main character, Sookie Stackhouse, has the ability to hear other people's thoughts, and we are occasionally made party to this, but with some sound distortion, to remind us that this is being processed for us through Sookie's telepathic powers. Often the technique is used to maximise the tension for the audience, particularly in the context of crime or horror narratives. In the film *The Silence of the Lambs* (1991), the scene where Clarice finally comes face to face with the serial killer Buffalo Bill is partly shot from the perspective of the killer who is wearing night vision glasses to allow him to see his victims in the dark. The idea of forcing the audience to share the perspective of the killer rather than the victim was also used famously and more controversially in the film *Peeping Tom* (1960), where the killer films his victims and plays back the films for his own sadistic gratification. The audience thus witnesses the act of killing through the lens of the killer's camera, with the effect of making us reflect on our position as voyeurs and making us question our roles and responsibilities as we are entertained by and even take pleasure in the suffering of others.

The ethical issues arising from the positioning of the viewer in relation to what he or she sees, and the extent to which viewers identify with what they are being shown, have been explored more fully in relation to cinematic narratives and the notion of scopophilia, spectatorship and voyeurism. We will return in the next chapter to issues relating to the responsibilities of narrators with regard to what they show and what they choose not to show their audiences and the extent to which this control over the story means we can only ever receive a partial or incomplete account. However, it should also be said that such techniques can be used for the purposes of humour. Both the British sitcom *Peep Show* (Channel 4, 2003–) and American comedy *Scrubs* (NBC/ABC 2001–10) have experimented with the use of voice-over and point-of-view shots to present the viewer with often discomfiting insights into the inner thoughts of their characters but played out in the familiar routines and settings which provide the 'situation' of this particular brand of comedy.

While the point-of-view shot can bring the viewer uncomfortably close to the perspective of one of the characters on screen, other techniques exist which perhaps place us more alongside rather than inside their perceptual fields. Julian Murphet (2005) uses the term 'associative focalization' where we 'associate the filmed perceptions with the face we see in successive shots . . . [to] fuse and form a single, complex image in the mind' (91). As opposed to direct focalization, here the viewer associates the emotions and reactions conveyed by a close-up on the face of one of the characters with objects in the shot, seeing those objects as though through the eyes of that face. The close-up also invites us as audience members to 'read' the emotions and psychological state of a character. Many soap operas end episodes with close-ups of characters, encouraging the viewer to speculate about the emotions they are going through as they react to the events unfolding.

With reference to some of the groundbreaking techniques used in *Citizen Kane* (1941), Seymour Chatman (1978) refers to instances where the 'actor can be so placed in the frame as to heighten our association with him' as 'perceptual sympathy', allowing for scenes in film whereby 'it is not always clear whether we have seen the object separately from the character, conjointly with him, or through him' (159). In both film and tv, the over-the-shoulder-shot can also be used to create the impression that we are sharing the physical trajectory of the character, for example, in a high-speed car chase. In Kubrick's film adaptation of Stephen King's *The Shining* (1980) we travel around the Overlook hotel as though on the shoulder of Danny, the camera tracking him as he rides his bike along the corridors. Shot as though from the eyeline of the little boy, the hotel seems even more creepy and mysterious, and the eerie effect is compounded by Kubrick's use of music and claustrophic set design.

FOCALIZATION AND IMMERSION

A fascination with penetrating through into the interior lives of others is something that is increasingly being seen as one of the main motivations behind our compulsion to tell and hear stories. In particular, cognitive narratology argues that narratives offer us the opportunity to read the minds of others, and to try to understand what it is like to experience the world differently. This seems to take us much further than simply thinking about how a reader or viewer is positioned and oriented in terms of actions and actors in a narrative. For example, David Herman (2002), drawing on possible worlds theory, introduced the term 'hypothetical focalization' to account for instances where the reader or audience is invited to consider what might have been seen had anyone been there to see it. Regardless of the means by which such insights and experiences are made possible, it seems we continually seek out 'expressive windows into the psychological life of sentient and affective beings' (Murphet 2005: 95) even animated creatures, nonhuman species or the supernatural.

Meanwhile, Bolter and Grusin (2000) have argued that narratives emerging from new media technologies push even further in the direction of offering audiences immersive experiences, with virtual reality headsets, Google Glass and 3D offering us the illusion of stepping into the world of the story or being surrounded by the creatures, sounds and sensations of a particular situation or environment.

VARIATIONS AND REVISIONS OF GENETTE'S THEORIES

Genette acknowledges that focalization in a narrative may be both variable, shifting between characters, and multiple, where the 'same' events may be presented from the point of view of different characters. He also accepts that 'Any single formula of focalization does not, therefore, always bear on an entire work, but rather on a definite narrative section, which can be very short' (1980: 191). Thus, in modernist fiction, for example, the novels of Virginia Woolf or James Joyce, focalization can shift between characters mid paragraph and even mid sentence, but it is the narrator who makes possible this dipping in and out of perspectives and who speaks and gives voice to the thoughts, feelings and beliefs of others. In a short story called 'Kew Gardens' (1919), Woolf plays with the idea of perspective in a sense close to that of a visual artist or even a filmmaker, representing the events of the story, the conversations taking place between visitors to the gardens, as though they are witnessed or overheard from within the flowerbeds as they pass by.

In revisiting Genette's terminology, Shlomith Rimmon-Kenan (1983) talks about focalization in terms of three facets: the perceptual (what the focalizer sees, hears etc); the psychological (what he or she is thinking or feeling); and the ideological (what he or she believes based on a particular worldview or value system). This allows for the possibility in narrative that we may share the perceptual field of one character (e.g. a child) while the moral evaluation of what we are seeing may be left to another character (e.g. a figure of authority or adult perhaps). While in many ways this is a welcome expansion of Genette's theory, it has proved especially controversial, because for some theorists (e.g. Chatman) such instances take us into the realm of narration, not focalization.

Following Mieke Bal, Rimmon-Kenan also departs from Genette's account of focalization to allow for the fact that a narrator may also be a focalizer and that focalization may be embedded in much the same way as narration. Dispensing with the notion of zero focalization, Bal and Rimmon-Kenan focus instead on the distinction between external and internal focalization. Internal focalization is where we share the point of view of a character, though Genette (1980) argues that 'it is rarely applied in a totally rigorous way' (192) other than in instances of interior monologue, where we seem party to a character's every sensation and thought. In Rimmon-Kenan's account, external focalization takes a position external to the storyworld and appears to be more 'objective' and less restricted than internal focalization.

Genette's theory isn't confined to the perceptual, but also takes into account the level of knowledge of the focalizer, allowing for the fact that even if this is limited the reader may still be able to read between the lines: 'Narrative always says less than it knows, but it often makes known more than it says' (198). In many accounts of Genette's theory no mention is made of this, leading in many instances to an attempt to be overly schematic in applying the terminology. The subjectivity, tentativeness of many narratives in conveying what a character may be thinking or feeling is thus lost, reducing the ambiguous, the paradoxical, the theoretically incompatible positions that Genette accepts as crucial to the style of his chosen subject, Proust's novel.

REPRESENTING SPEECH AND THOUGHT

As part of her discussion of narration, Rimmon-Kenan (1983) considers the various techniques available to the writer when it comes to representing what others say or think. She does so in relation to the distinction between diegesis and mimesis that goes back to classical antiquity, and which relates to the degree to which the writer takes responsibility for what is being reported. Popularised as 'telling' versus 'showing', mimesis is where the storyteller steps back from the scene as though *directly* showing or reporting what was said. At the other extreme, the storyteller offers only his or her *indirect* account of what was said. In this sense, the representation of speech and thought is intertwined with the degree or mediation or intervention imposed by the storyteller.

In typologies of speech presentation (Rimmon-Kenan 1983; Leech and Short 1981) terms such as 'free' and 'direct' can convey the impression that somehow fiction can offer us unmediated access to the speech or thought of others. Thus in novels such as Irvine Welsh's *Trainspotting* (1995), the characters' speech seems so gritty and uncompromising it is as though it is taken directly from the streets. However, even here we see that the representation may be heavily stylised, with frequent repetition of idioms and phrases to help the reader identify the characters, and with the characters seemingly being at pains to observe all the niceties of polite discourse with one another, never interrupting or talking over one another, even in the most heated of exchanges. Even where speech seems most 'real' to us, what we have is an imitation of speech: behind the words of the fictional character we have the figure of the implied author (see Chapter 4), shaping and framing that speech for us (Thomas 2012).

Challenging the speech category approach of Leech and Short amongst others, Palmer (2004) argues that it is too simplistic to simply carry over the same typology from speech to thought. In addition, he challenges the assumption that where a writer focuses on action and spoken interaction it means that the reader cannot engage with what the participants may be thinking or feeling. Palmer has also demonstrated that in certain novels (one of his main examples is George Eliot's *Middlemarch*) such is the focus on an ensemble of characters, a social milieu, that it is even possible to speak of a 'social mind' in action.

Though many accounts of narration and point of view make no reference to the representation of speech and thought, as Genette (1980) claimed in his study, experimentation with such techniques have become 'one of the main paths of emancipation in the modern novel' (173). From the modernists onwards, writers have experimented with ways of capturing the idioms and nuances of spoken interactions, and the flights and complexities of our inner thoughts and desires. In the fields of narratology, stylistics and literary criticism, of particular interest is **free indirect discourse** (see, for example, Leech and Short 1981), described as the combination of two voices, although it may actually combine many more than two voices, where a narrator's representation of events is coloured by the perspective of one or more characters. Who speaks and who sees in such passages can be a matter of intense debate and discussion. For some, indirect or quasi-direct representations of speech and thought are a particular feature of the novel and its innate dialogicity (Bakhtin 1981), whereby every voice and every utterance echoes with the voices and utterances of others. However, more recently, studies have shown that discourses such as advertising and journalism also make use of free indirect discourse (e.g. Jeffries 2009), drawing us into the inner worlds of participants in a very subtle and unobtrusive way.

CONCLUSION

Representing the voices and perspectives of others plays an important role in any story and is crucial to a narrative's ability to engage, thrill and move the reader or viewer. As we shall see in the next chapter, while this representation may be manipulated for the purpose of persuading us and shaping our responses, equally it can be seen as a way of devolving control and power in a narrative, giving up the telling of the story to a whole multitude of different possibilities, opening it up to potentially conflicting interpretations. An analysis of the role of narration, focalization and the representation of speech and thought will be combined with an ideological analysis of a news story in the next chapter.

FOLLOW-UP ACTIVITIES

1. Rewrite the opening to a novel written in the first person in the third person. Examples might include the opening to *The Catcher in the Rye* (1951) by J. D. Salinger or *The Buddha of Suburbia* (1990) by Hanif Kureishi. Consider how these changes affect our response to the events and individuals depicted and our confidence in the truth or authenticity of the narrative.

   Alternatively, take a news story and rewrite events from the perspective of one of the participants (e.g. an eyewitness, a victim's family member etc.).

2. Reimagine a scene from a tv show or film, representing an alternative point of view to the original. For example, you might focus on what a minor or peripheral character sees or hears. In a crime or horror drama, you could show events from the point of view of the victim rather than the murderer.

SUGGESTED READING

Genette's *Narrative Discourse* remains the key text in terms of providing us with a vocabulary for the different kinds of narrative voice available to writers of literary fiction. As indicated above, many of his concepts and terms have also been applied to other narrative media, especially film. For specific discussions of the concept of narration in relation to film, and comparisons between film and prose fiction, Seymour Chatman's *Story and Discourse: Narrative Structure in Fiction and Film* provides a very readable and insightful account, taking issue with some of the assumptions made by Genette and others about the distinction between narration and point of view. Edward Branigan's *Narrative Comprehension and Film* is more deeply rooted in film studies, and draws on linguistics and cognitive science as well as classical narratology. For a discussion of framing, see my entry in *The Encyclopedia of the Novel* or Chapter 3, on the borders of narrative, in Porter Abbott's book.

As suggested above, a number of often conflicting accounts of point of view and focalization exist. In my view, when first studying this complex subject, it is a good idea to stick to one theory and one set of terms. I have used Shlomith Rimmon-Kenan's *Narrative Fiction: Contemporary Poetics* for many years in my classes. It provides a good distillation and refinement of some of Genette's terms, and also considers the representation of speech and thought in some depth.

Julian Murphet's chapters on voice and point of view in *Narrative and Media* provide an excellent discussion of the issues in relation to the analysis of classic and contemporary media, from Hitchcock's *Rebecca* to *Fight Club* and *Monsters, Inc.* David Ciccoricco has written about point of view in relation to digital fiction with particular reference to multimodality and the intervention of the reader. For a discussion of Genette's terms in relation to comics, see Julia Round's article 'Visual Perspective and Narrative Voice in Comics'.

For discussion of the representation of speech and thought, Leech and Short's *Style in Fiction* remains a key text. Drawing on this typology, stylisticians such as Jeffries have analysed free indirect discourse and other techniques in news stories and political discourse, while Sara Mills discusses focalization and the representation of speech and thought in relation to advertising.

REFERENCES

Abbott, H.P. (2008) (2nd ed.) *The Cambridge Introduction to Narrative*. Cambridge: Cambridge University Press.

Bakhtin, M. (1981) *The Dialogic Imagination*. Transl. C. Emerson and M. Holquist. Austin: University of Texas Press.

Bolter, J. and Grusin, R. (2000) *Remediation: Understanding New Media*. Cambridge, MA: MIT Press.

Branigan, E. (1992) *Narrative Comprehension and Film*. London: Routledge.

Chatman, S. (1978) *Story and Discourse: Narrative Structure in Fiction and Film*. Ithaca: Cornell University Press.

Chatman, S. (1990) *Coming to Terms: The Rhetoric of Narrative in Fiction and Film*. Ithaca: Cornell University Press.

Ciccoricco, D. (2014) Digital Fiction and Worlds of Perspective. In *Analyzing Digital Fiction*, eds. A. Bell, A. Ensslin and H. Rustad. London: Routledge, 39–56.

Genette, G. (1980) *Narrative Discourse*. Transl. J.E. Lewin. Ithaca: Cornell University Press.

Golding, W. (1956) *Pincher Martin*. London: Faber and Faber.

Herman, D. (2002) *Story Logic: Problems and Possibilities of Narrative*. Lincoln: University of Nebraska Press.

Jahn, M. (2005) Focalization. In *Routledge Encyclopedia of Narrative*, eds. D. Herman, M-L. Ryan and M. Jahn. London: Routledge, 173–7.

Jeffries, L. (2009) *Critical Stylistics*. Basingstoke: Palgrave Macmillan.

Lanser, S. (1981) *The Narrative Act: Point of View in Prose Fiction*. Princeton: Princeton University Press.

Leech, G. and Short, M.H. (1981) *Style in Fiction*. Harlow: Longman.

Mills, S. (1995) *Feminist Stylistics*. London: Routledge.

Murphet, J. (2005) Narrative Time. Narrative Voice. Point of View. In *Narrative and Media*, ed. H. Fulton. Cambridge: Cambridge University Press, 60–95.

Ong, W. (1982) *Orality and Literacy: The Technologizing of the Word*. London: Methuen.

Palmer, A. (2004) *Fictional Minds*. Lincoln: University of Nebraska Press.

Richardson, B. (2006) *Unnatural Voices: Extreme Narration in Modern and Contemporary Fiction*. Columbus: Ohio State University Press.

Rimmon-Kenan, S. (1983) *Narrative Fiction: Contemporary Poetics*. London: Methuen.

Round, J. (2007) Visual Perspective and Narrative Voice in Comics: Redefining Literary Terms. *International Journal of Comic Art*, 9(2), 316–29.

Ryan, M-L. (1990) Stacks, Frames and Boundaries, or Narrative as Computer Language. *Poetics Today*, 11(4), 873–99.

Thomas, B. (2011) Frame. In *The Encyclopedia of the Novel*, ed. P. Logan. Malden, MA: Wiley Blackwell, 320–25.

Thomas, B. (2012) *Fictional Dialogue: Speech and Conversation in the Modern and Postmodern Novel*. Lincoln: University of Nebraska Press.

Thomas, B. (2014) 140 Characters in Search of a Story: Twitterfiction as an Emerging Narrative Form. In *Analyzing Digital Fiction*, eds. A. Bell and A. Ensslin. London: Routledge.

4

NARRATIVE AND IDEOLOGY

'Narratives are . . . a kind of political action.'

(Toolan 2001: 206)

Ideology = 'any system of values based on ideas or prejudices and cultural and social assumptions which amounts to a pervasive, unconscious, world-view.'

(Wales 2001: 196)

In the last chapter we looked at some of the ways in which the telling of the tale, or its 'angle of vision' (Rimmon-Kenan 1983: 71), filters, shapes and even skews what we see, feel and believe. In earlier chapters we looked at recurring patterns in narrative and the idea that there may even be a universal structure for narrative that can be found across cultures and stretching from our earliest history to the narratives we produce today. It is clear, therefore, that narrative is a potentially powerful force, and that stories can be used to persuade and steer us towards accepting certain values and beliefs as the norm. This is not simply a case of seeing narrative as the transmission of beliefs and ideas, but of recognising narrative as a 'mode of thinking' (Tambling 1991: 109), shaping the way we conceptualise our experiences, for example, in terms of discrete 'events', with a causal logic making them relatable and meaningful rather than random and disconnected.

Narrative is also often explicitly concerned with worldbuilding and imagining social structures and ways of organising culture and society that may act as a critique of what exists in the real world. A focus on the relationship between narrative and ideology takes us beyond the text to consider how cultural representations engage with the politics of class, race, gender and so on.

In this chapter we will consider Marxist approaches to the study of narrative and the extent to which narratives are seen as perpetuating dominant **ideologies** and even duping or misleading their audiences. The chapter will also look at rhetorical approaches to the study of narrative where issues of control and responsibility for the story are often to the fore. However, the chapter will also examine counterarguments to these approaches, considering whether narrative forms may in fact present us with an array of viewpoints and positions, some of which contradict and challenge dominant ideologies in a way that can be potentially empowering for audiences. This will open the way for a discussion of active readers/audiences, to be explored more fully in Chapter 5.

MARXIST APPROACHES TO NARRATIVE

According to classical Marxism, ideology works in the interests of the dominant class, whose ownership of the modes of production (film companies, publishers, tv stations) means they can control what values and beliefs are given expression. At its most extreme, for example, in the work of the Frankfurt School, cultural texts are seen a means of oppression, of social control. In fact, popular forms of entertainment are seen as a means of distracting the masses from their own oppression and seducing them with the lure of short-term material gain. A Marxist approach might therefore focus on how advertisements promote bourgeois domesticity or how quiz shows and ads help to encourage rampant consumerism. However, the pessimism of the Frankfurt school, and the idea that audiences are obedient and helpless in the face of social control, has increasingly been questioned by cultural commentators.

Classical Marxist approaches have fallen out of favour in recent years, replaced by analyses which focus more on identity formation and the politics of gender, ethnicity and so on. Nevertheless, in media studies in particular, analysis of particular narrative forms is often situated within discussions of specific industrial and political contexts and a recognition that 'It is impossible to stand outside ideology and talk about it in a language which is itself free of ideology' (Turner 2006: 198). Media and film studies also resolutely retains a focus on forms of representation as a kind of social practice that affects ordinary people's everyday lives.

Ideology as it is understood in most contemporary studies of media narratives owes much more to Althusser and Gramsci than to Marx. In particular, Althusser's (1971) definition of ideology as 'a representation of the imaginary relationship of individuals to their real conditions of existence' (152) shifted the focus onto issues of representation and how cultural texts help us to make sense of the world and our place in it. Althusser's conception of ideology is of something that is both complex and contradictory, and in his account, rather than being passive dupes of dominant ideologies, individuals take up the subject positions offered to them by the powerful social forces or 'ideological state apparatuses' in society, including the church, the family and the media. According to Althusser, the subject is continuously interpellated or 'hailed' by cultural texts such as advertisements so that we come to recognise ourselves as 'the family man', 'the singleton', 'the career woman' and so on according to the specific subject positions that these texts offer us. Ideology thus offers the individual a sense of coherence and belonging and relies on the individual's complicity in perpetuating his or her oppression by the system.

As well as allowing for the possibility of resistance, Gramsci's theory of negotiated hegemony has paved the way for cultural studies theorists to focus on the potential for the negotiation of meaning (discussed in Chapter 5) and for the possibility that cultural texts not only provide the means for oppression, but of liberation, particularly with regard to the liberation of ordinary people's voices (Lewis 2002: 99). In the work of Dick Hebdige (1979) on youth subcultures or John Fiske (1987) on television cultures and active audiences, we see a shift away from Marxist tirades against the dominance of the mass media or the hopelessly passive consumer, towards understanding the ways in which social groups can respond with subversion and creativity to the cultural texts they encounter.

Fiske and Hartley (1978) argued that the tv show *Come Dancing*, popular in the UK in the 1970s, could be read as a contemporary take on the Cinderella fable. They claimed that the glittering costumes, the heavy makeup and the choreographed routines conveyed to the audience the myth of social mobility, offering the illusion that the contestants could step outside of their social class, only to be called back to reality at the stroke of midnight, returning to the working-class communities from whence they came.

Strictly Come Dancing (BBC, 2004–) is a popular contemporary reworking of the format, but this time with celebrities as contestants. The show still plays heavily on the idea of glamour, but it is perhaps more a reflection on contemporary ideologies of celebrity than of class. Most of the contestants are on the show to promote or resuscitate their careers, and while many have existing fan bases that ensure their success in the competition, part of the appeal of the show is seeing these celebrities taken out of their comfort zones and being ritually humiliated by the judges. In the updated format, viewers can vote on the performances and override the judges' opinions, and in some instances the audience in fact may be said to subvert and even derail the show. In 2008, the distinctly inelegant political correspondent John Sergeant was repeatedly voted back in by viewers; he eventually bowed out of his own accord because he felt that winning the show would be 'a joke too far' (http://news.bbc.co.uk/1/hi/7737447.stm). Openly contradicting the judgement of the panel of experts, the audience thus seemed to be defying the ethos of the show and mocking the illusion behind the competitive façade that success is built on hard work and determination. According to Gramsci's theory of hegemony, resistance to dominant ideologies is possible, but eventually that resistance is itself incorporated by the dominant class and made safe. Far from threatening the success of the show, therefore, the audience's support for the underdog itself became one of its talking points, not exactly encouraged but turned into a joke by the show's hosts and producers, with Sergeant's departure paving the way for a reestablishment of the status quo as an actor from the popular medical drama *Holby City* (BBC, 1999–) went on to become the 'deserving' winner.

Television narratives perhaps offer the most compelling examples of the complex interplay between ideology and resistance, particularly in an era where new technologies appear to offer audiences more of a say and a voice. This has been a main focus of studies of talk shows and reality television, where marginalised and disenfranchised groups are often the subjects of the discussion or narrative. For some, this can be empowering, as new voices and new stories are given airtime. However, others are critical of the 'freakshow' (Dovey 2000) mentality that this can encourage, where participants are paraded in front of the audience only so that we may mock and feel superior to them. In the UK in 2014, the term 'poverty porn' was used widely in the press following the furore over the broadcast of a series called *Benefits Street* on Channel 4. Despite the show's claims to present the reality of life for people living on benefits in contemporary Britain, many criticised its representation of the participants as pandering to the stereotype that those who depend on benefits are scroungers and criminals.

In the field of literary criticism, early Marxist theory focused on the representation of social class in literary fiction and the extent to which texts reflected the social reality of the time in which they were written. However, with the work of Pierre Macherey (1978) the idea that ideology is full of gaps opened up a new kind of analysis in which what the text does *not* say or what it represses became just as important as identifying the ideological positions it seems to put forward. More recently, cultural materialism and new historicism focus on the constructive role of ideology in shaping individual subjects as well as societies. New historicism considers literary texts alongside the nonliterary, while a cultural materialist approach is characterised by writing that wears its political commitments and beliefs on its sleeve and challenges not only the ideologies represented *in* literary texts, but the very practices and modes of reading that have dominated the study of literature.

BARTHES'S MYTHOLOGIES

Roland Barthes's work on contemporary mass media mythologies also helped to shape and influence the emerging focus on ideology and the politics of representation. In the mid-1950s, Barthes published an essay a month 'trying to reflect regularly on some myths of French daily life' (Preface, 1993[1957]: 11). His motivation was his frustration at exposing the '*what-goes-without-saying*, the ideological abuse' (emphasis in original, 11) which he saw in the French press of the time, naturalising a view of reality which was ideological, and presenting as the only reality what Barthes called 'the falsely obvious' (11).

Taking as his subjects contemporary advertising, film, sport and cuisine, Barthes offered readings of everyday myths so as to demystify the ways in which seemingly harmless and innocuous cultural signs and practices contributed to an interrelated system of meanings or mythology which in plain sight carried out the work of bourgeois ideology and French imperialism.

Barthes's theory of myth brought a new political dimension to narratology, moving away from more traditional notions of myth as reflecting shared needs and shared realities, to embrace 'the contradictions of [his] time' and the role of myth in transitory and fragmented urban societies. *Mythologies* helped to establish semiotics as a key conceptual and methodological framework for the analysis of contemporary media texts. Barthes's concept of myth has been applied widely to television narratives (Fiske and Hartley 1978; Masterman 1984) and to advertisements (Williamson 1978). In 2013, a new volume celebrating 50 or so years since the publication of Barthes's original essays explored contemporary myths ranging from the Higgs boson particle and press freedom to the zombie walk and Australian pop star Kylie Minogue.

Despite the fact that Barthes's focus in this aspect of his work was so clearly ideological, narratology, especially structuralist narratology, has been dismissed by many as being so concerned with form, language and structure as to be blind to the social context from which signs and structures derive their meaning. However, as narratology has responded to poststructuralism and the influence of critical approaches such as feminism and postcolonialism, the term contextual narratology has emerged in opposition to formalist narratology and as part of a seeming advance into a 'postclassical' phase.

RHETORICAL APPROACHES

The notion of narrative as 'a purposive communicative act' (Phelan 2007: 203) where the intention is to influence the reader or audience goes back to the very earliest attempts to account for the effects that narrative may have on us. The rhetorical approach to narrative is said to have its roots in Aristotle's *Poetics*, and particularly the notion that art is cathartic, arousing pity and fear in its audience in a purging of the emotions, the effect of which is felt long after the acting out of the story or the reading of the book. According to this view of narrative, the telling of the story and the particular choices made in the narration have 'designs on its audience's values' (Phelan 2007: 208), not necessarily to the extent of indoctrination that a Marxist theorist may claim, but with full recognition of the fact that story-tellers seek to shape and influence their audiences. The role of the narrator is crucial in this respect, often acting as a moral lodestone for the reader, evaluating events and offering a moral perspective. But the rhetorical approach is careful to distinguish between author and narrator, and between author and 'implied author' (Booth 1961), or the version of him or herself that the author presents in the narrative. Thus authors may signal the extent to which they endorse or depart from the views of the tale's narrator(s), indicating their reliability or otherwise as guides to the action.

In Phelan's recent championing of the rhetorical approach, the issue of ethics has become more and more prominent. In highlighting the importance of ethical values for narrative, this view sees narrative as being less about a unidirectional flow of meanings from a source of authority (narrator) to a passive receptacle (reader) than being about something that carries with it responsibilities on either side. Some (e.g. Altes 2005: 142) have even argued for an 'ethical turn' in narrative theory, seeing narrative as providing us with the opportunity to exercise moral judgements and make ethical choices, not so much as to promote predetermined conclusions, but to encourage the development of interpretive and discursive skills. An ethical reading does not entail mindlessly subscribing to a text's ideological stance, but rather 'does justice to the appeal made by the text' (Herman and Vervaek 2007: 219), giving due respect to the stance offered.

DIALOGISM

In his influential theory of the novel, the Russian theorist Mikhail Bakhtin argued that narrative may offer contesting positions and voices rather than a monologic stance where all the text's voices are subordinate to that of the author. In the dialogic text, there is a continuous interplay between voices, a kind of 'verbal give-and-take' (1981: 314) where the narrator's own discourse may appear as just one amongst many. According to Bakhtin, the novel offers readers a unique opportunity to come 'to know one's own belief system in someone else's belief system' (365), so that every position or stance comes to be seen as contestable and capable of entering into dialogue with other perspectives and other positions. Bakhtin's concept of the novel as embracing the coexistence of competing voices allows us to talk about narrative as a site for the display of power while also accepting the possibility for openness and resistance, and has been very influential not only on theories of the novel or literary and linguistic criticism, but also on film, media and cultural studies. In many ways, Bakhtin's work can be seen as pivotal in allowing theorists to argue that texts may in fact promote and encourage active readers and audiences by foregrounding competing voices and refusing to subsume these to some kind of overarching ideology. In the next chapter, our attention will turn to the role of the reader and to recent work which suggest that contemporary narratives, particularly in the digital sphere, can offer more and more opportunities for audiences to have their say, but also to help shape, influence and even create narratives themselves.

POSTMODERNISM AND THE POSTIDEOLOGICAL

Postmodernism is often characterised and caricatured as a rejection of the possibility of belief or faith in institutions and dominant discourses that purport to offer us absolute truths of any kind. In *The Postmodern Condition*, Lyotard (1984) explicitly attacks what he calls 'metanarratives' which seem to legitimise certain meanings and truths. These **grand or master narratives** could include religious, scientific or historical systems of knowledge, which would once have had considerable power, but which in contemporary society are challenged more and more by 'little narratives' which seek their legitimation locally rather than universally (McHale 1992: 20).

Slavoj Zizek (1989) explores whether this loss of faith or belief in institutions and systems of knowledge means we are now a 'postideological' society. Fundamental Marxist notions such as that of false consciousness do not make sense, Zizek argues, if there is no Truth to reveal behind the false representations, just as the idea of ideology as some kind of illusion or mask doesn't make sense if nobody ever believes that they are dupes of ideology, only other people. For postmodern society, Zizek (1989) suggests, we need to rewrite the Marxian formula 'they do not know it, but they are doing it', to read instead 'they know what they are doing, and they are doing it' (33).

Žižek's often playful and provocative approach to examining these issues can be complex and frustrating, but in his reexamination of some of the fundamental tenets of Marxism, coupled with his exploration of the politics of psychoanalytical theory, he has provided some entertaining and fascinating insights, especially into film narratives and the ideological fantasies they rely on.

ANALYSIS

News stories have been a major focus for ideological criticism because they often deal directly with political issues, and because the particular take on events they offer is so clearly shaped and defined by the interests and leanings of the owners of news corporations. A common strategy is to compare how the 'same' story is represented in tabloid and broadsheet newspapers or in newspapers representing different political interests. Linguistic criticism of such stories might focus on the particular terms of address used for those caught up in the story, for example, whether they are 'protestors' or 'rioters', 'insurgents' or 'terrorists'. Language can also shape how blame and responsibility is apportioned, for example, whether individuals or organisations are seen to be directly responsible for events. Thus, depending on how a sentence is composed we may be left in no doubt as to who did what to whom ('The police removed protestors from the site'), whereas using a passive construction leaves much more room for ambiguity ('Protestors were removed at dawn').

News stories do not have narrators in the same sense as works of fiction, but nevertheless choices are made about how the story is told and whose voices are represented. For example, a story may foreground the reactions of those involved, whether protestors complaining about their mistreatment or the police explaining their actions as a response to provocation. Campaigns such as Who Makes the News (WMTN; www.whomakesthenews.org) highlight the ways in which some voices are repeatedly marginalised or excluded, in this case the voices of women.

The structure of news stories can also help to reinforce a particular ideological view, for example, in terms of what our culture deems to be newsworthy. News stories traditionally start with the most recent events and work backwards. So the attention of the reader is on what has just happened and on the outcome to events rather than on the process leading up to the crime, the attack or the disaster.

THE DISAPPEARANCE OF FLIGHT MH370

One of the biggest news stories in the spring of 2014 concerned the mysterious disappearance of flight MH370 with over 200 passengers on board. For weeks, news sources speculated about the possible causes for the disappearance, including hijacking and terrorism, while wilder theories of the plane's whereabouts circulated freely across social media platforms such as Twitter. The similarities between the story and the plot of the hit American TV show *Lost* only fuelled this speculation: in the TV show an airplane crashes on a mysterious island, with sinister corporations, mythical creatures and complex character backstories all contributing to a drama which kept viewers guessing right up until the end. Interest in the story meant it was widely reported and remained high on the agendas of both print and television news sources across the globe. The Malaysian authorities gave daily briefings and came under increasing scrutiny and suspicion as the relatives of the missing expressed their concerns and frustrations at the slow progress of the investigation. On 24 March 2014, the Malaysian authorities announced that the evidence now suggested that the plane was in fact lost and that all on board had perished.

The following report appeared on the website of the British newspaper *The Guardian* the day after the announcement. A daily broadsheet newspaper, *The Guardian* is regarded as a newspaper that provides in-depth reports on international politics and current affairs, and is not afraid to carry out probing and sometimes controversial investigations into government organisations and big business.

> Malaysia Airlines officials offered their 'prayers and sincere condolences' to family members of passengers on board flight MH370 after authorities said they had concluded that the missing plane crashed in the remote Indian Ocean with the loss of all 239 people on board.
>
> Grief-stricken families and friends marched on the Malaysian embassy in Beijing after being given the news by Malaysian authorities.
>
> The Malaysia Airlines group chief executive officer, Ahmad Jauhari Yahya, said at a press conference: 'My heart breaks to think of the

unimaginable pain suffered by all the families. There are no words which can ease that pain.'

'Everyone in the Malaysia Airlines family is praying for the 239 souls on MH370 and for their loved ones on this dark day. We extend our prayers and sincere condolences.'

Yahya added that whether or not he would resign was 'a personal question' that he would consider later.

(Accessed 24/3/15 at http://www.theguardian.com/world/2014/mar/25/mh370-airline-prayers-condolences-all-hope-lost)

On the day that the story broke, news corporations were accused by some of showing a lack of sensitivity to the families of the victims. It was also widely reported that protests in China were directed at the Malaysian authorities, accusing them of trying to 'delay, distort and hide the truth' (http://www.bbc.co.uk/news/world-asia-26728045). In the UK, both the BBC and the *Daily Mail* carried stories focusing on a UK firm's role in helping to track down the airplane, and both the BBC and *The Guardian* featured stories about some of the Australian families caught up in the disaster. This reflects the importance of analysing news stories in the context of news values (Galtung and Ruge 1965) and understanding that the newsworthiness of a story is culturally variable. Thus prominence tends to be given to bad news over good, to stories that have cultural proximity for the readership/audience and to stories that offer continuity, spanning weeks and maybe even months. In the case of the reporting of the fate of flight MH370, the event clearly had the virtue of being unexpected and momentous, and the daily updates ensured that the story remained fresh. However, for UK audiences it presumably was felt that a focus on the UK firm and on Australian citizens was necessary to sustain interest and a sense of identification. Implicit in much of the reporting of the event was a suspicion that the Malaysian authorities were concealing information, and that it was the involvement of the West that would finally lead to the mystery being resolved.

In the extract, we can see that the reporting provides some degree of personalisation in the form of the emotive and highly personal response of the airline official. He is quoted directly, with the emotion and religious register ('prayers'; 'souls') of his words given prominence through repetition. Meanwhile the responses of the 'grief stricken families and friends' are only hinted at obliquely, keeping us somewhat at a distance. The statement of the unspecified 'authorities' relating to the disaster is similarly reported indirectly. It could be argued that this is a way of distancing us as readers from the authorities who are as remote as the region in which the plane reportedly crashed, and instead Yahya seems to shoulder the responsibility (if not the blame) for the disaster. The idea of the airline as a 'family' is highly ideological, suggesting that they are a caring and protective organisation rather than a cold and heartless corporation. But the reporting of the events also uses highly expressive language ('marched'), subtly conveying the sense of outrage and anger felt by the families as well as their powerlessness ('given the news by Malaysian authorities'). In fact, other news sources (e.g. *The Washington Post*) reported that the news was sent by text (SMS) message to the families, heightening the sense felt by many that the authorities in question were afraid to confront the truth of the situation.

Close analysis of news stories highlights the importance of what might seem like fairly trivial choices in naming individuals. For example, the Malaysian Airline's official's full name is given, as is his job title, while later in the story the use of his surname only connotes his authority (as opposed to using his first name, which would suggest intimacy). In the case of reporting on disasters of this kind, it is perhaps understandable that news organisations want to avoid speculation and rely on official sources as being the most likely to offer accurate information. Nevertheless, as we have seen, subtle choices in language, structure and style betray a particular view of events which restricts the range of possibilities for how they may be interpreted by the reader.

CONCLUSION

News stories are expected to report events objectively, and often draw on the same sources (e.g. agency reports, press releases), especially for breaking or international news. Nevertheless, an ideological analysis exposes how language and structure help to shape and direct the reader or viewer's response and can also highlight what is *not* said as well as what is. Whereas traditional news sources such as broadsheet newspapers and public service broadcasters still command respect and appear authoritative, this does not meant that their readers and audiences are incapable of questioning their reporting of events. Newspapers have always included comment pieces, editorials and features that offer more divergent opinions. In the age of the internet, 'citizen journalists' may report on events via blogs and websites, challenging official news sources and traditional gatekeepers, while social media and comment sections offer readers the opportunity to react to what is being reported and to interact with journalists and other readers. The changing perceptions of readers and audiences and the platforms for response available to them will be explored more fully in the next chapter and in Chapter 8.

SUGGESTED READING

Mimi White's chapter 'Ideological Analysis' provides an excellent overview of classical Marxism and ideology in relation to contemporary television narratives. Another good introduction is provided in Jeff Lewis's chapter 'Marxism and the Formation of Cultural Ideology'. Jeremy Tambling's *Narrative and Ideology* focuses more closely on written narratives and pays close attention to *how* ideologies are perpetuated and challenged in novels and short stories. Close analysis of the language of news reporting is offered in Michael Toolan's study and in Paul Simpson's book on point of view. A more explicitly narratological discussion may be found in Luc Herman and Bart Vervaeck's chapter on Ideology in *The Cambridge Companion to Narrative*.

John Fiske's *Reading Television* and *Television Culture* both offer Barthesian readings of contemporary cultural forms, while Bennett and McDougall's volume of essays, *Barthes' 'Mythologies' Today* demonstrates Barthes's continued importance to cultural criticism. Finally, the documentary *The Pervert's Guide to Cinema* (2006) is a wonderful introduction to Žižek's work and a fascinating insight into the symbols and techniques used by some of the great directors, including Alfred Hitchcock.

REFERENCES

Altes, L.K. (2005) Ethical Turn. In *Routledge Encyclopedia of Narrative Theory*, eds. D. Herman, M. Jahn and M-L. Ryan. London: Routledge, 142–6.

Althusser, L. (1971) *Lenin and Philosophy and Other Essays*. London: New Left Books.

Bakhtin, M. (1981) *The Dialogic Imagination*. Transl. C. Emerson and M. Holquist. Austin: University of Texas Press.

Barthes, R. (1993[1957]) *Mythologies*. Transl. A. Lavers. London: Vintage.

Bennett, P. and McDougall, J. (2013) *Barthes' 'Mythologies' Today: Readings of Contemporary Culture*. London: Routledge.

Booth, W.C. (1961) *The Rhetoric of Fiction*. Chicago: Chicago University Press.

Dovey, J. (2000) *Freakshow: First Person Media and Factual Television*. London: Pluto Press.

Fiske, J. (1987) *Television Culture*. London: Routledge.

Fiske, J. and Hartley, J. (1978) *Reading Television*. London: Methuen.

Galtung, J. and Ruge, M. (1965) The Structure of Foreign News. *Journal of International Peace Research*, 1, 64–91.

Gramsci, A. (1971) *Selections from the Prison Notebooks*. Transl. Q. Hoare and G. Nowell-Smith. London: Lawrence & Wishart.

Hebdige, D. (1979) *Subculture: The Meaning of Style*. London: Methuen.

Herman, L. and Vervaek, B. (2007) Ideology. In *The Cambridge Companion to Narrative*, ed. D. Herman. Cambridge: Cambridge University Press, 217–30.

Lewis, J. (2002) *Cultural Studies: The Basics*. London: Sage.

Lyotard, J. (1984) *The Postmodern Condition*. Transl. G. Bennington and B. Massumi. Minneapolis: University of Minnesota Press.

Macherey, P. (1978) *A Theory of Literary Production*. Transl. G. Wall. London: Routledge and Kegan Paul.

Masterman, L. (ed.) (1984) *Television Mythologies*. London: Comedia.

McHale, B. (1992) *Constructing Postmodernism*. London: Routledge.

Phelan, J. (2007) Rhetoric/Ethics. In *The Cambridge Companion to Narrative*, ed. D. Herman. Cambridge: Cambridge University Press, 203–16.

Rimmon-Kenan, S. (1983) *Narrative Fiction: Contemporary Poetics*. London: Methuen.

Simpson, P. (1993) *Language, Ideology and Point of View*. London: Routledge.

Tambling, J. (1991) *Narrative and Ideology*. Milton Keynes: Open University Press.

Toolan, M. (2001) (2nd ed.) *Narrative: A Critical Linguistic Introduction*. London: Routledge.

Turner, G. (2006) *Film as Social Practice*. London: Routledge.

Wales, K. (2001) (2nd ed.) *A Dictionary of Stylistics*. Harlow: Longman.

White, M. (1992) Ideological Analysis and Television. In *Channels of Discourse: Reassembled*, ed. R.C. Allen. London: Routledge, 161–202.

Williamson, J. (1978) *Decoding Advertisements*. London: Marion Boyars.

Žižek, S. (1989) *The Sublime Object of Ideology*. London: Verso.

5

THE ROLE OF THE READER

'The birth of the reader must be at the cost of the death of the Author.'

(Barthes 1977: 148)

'Texts don't *contain* meaning but are *made* to mean as readers/viewers encounter them.'

(Allen 1992: 133)

While the reader is often left out of narratological accounts or is dealt with only as an abstraction, audiences have been a central focus in media, film and cultural studies for many years, and the emergence of Web 2.0 has meant that it is easier than ever to capture and engage with the views and responses of readers online. In literary criticism, the reader is almost always an abstraction, and feminists have long railed against the tendency to use the generic 'he' even where the readerships of certain genres or authors are widely known to be predominantly female. Approaches to studying readers derived from literary studies have tended to focus on how the reader may be (re)constructed from textual cues, with the notable exception of empirical approaches where the behaviour and affective responses of readers may be central. In media studies, ethnographic methods and less obtrusive recording devices made it possible to capture the behaviour of audience members in increasingly naturalistic contexts, as in Morley's (1986) study of families watching television shows in the 1980s. More recently, data capture tools for social media and website traffic make it possible to gather vast amounts of information about the habits and proclivities of readers and viewers, allowing media corporations not just to record but also predict where the next big hit may come from. This chapter will explore some of the foundational studies of readers and audiences demonstrating how many of their terms and models have proven useful for analysing practices and technologies far beyond what they could have imagined.

BARTHES AND THE ROLE OF THE READER

THE DEATH OF THE AUTHOR

In one of his most well-known essays, Barthes (1977) controversially proclaimed the 'Death of the Author' claiming that this was a necessary step allowing for the 'birth' or liberation of the reader. As so often, Barthes's language is highly figurative, suggestive here of revolution, and he presents the overthrow of the author figure as a political act not just against an individual but a whole 'empire'. Barthes argues that the idea of the author as an all-knowing figure or inspired genius who owns the text's meanings is a product of a capitalist ideology that privileges the individual over the collective. In the Middle Ages, texts were produced collectively and the idea of copying someone else's work would not have been perceived as stealing or doing something unlawful. Similarly, the text would not have been conceived of as an object or commodity, but as something that is always in process.

Barthes proposes an alternative term, the 'scriptor', who exists only in amongst the 'tissue of quotations' which is the text and which is 'drawn from the centres of culture' (146). The reading and interpretation of texts is similarly transformed, from a process of uncovering the meaning hidden *in* the text, towards seeing the text as something that is open, incapable of 'ultimate' meanings or meanings that can be 'arrested'. The role of the reader becomes central as 'a text's unity lies not in its origin but in its destination' (148), reversing the neglect of classical criticism in a move that is truly revolutionary.

THE PLEASURE OF THE TEXT

In another essay Barthes (1975a) employs the language of desire and the erotic to try to put into words different kinds of reading pleasure. On the one hand, Barthes argues, we have 'plaisir', a safe and reassuring experience that is familiar and unthreatening. But texts can also produce a more disturbing, violent kind of pleasure ('jouissance') which escapes any kind of control, and produces a kind of ecstasy or bliss in the reader. As such, jouissance can pose a threat to the idea of order or control and (along with Lacan's use of the term) has been seized on in particular by feminist critics and theorists as a way of articulating the possibility of subverting dominant meanings and of reinscribing reading (and writing) as an embodied activity.

Barthes's work on the pleasure of the text seems to offer a way of understanding popular culture as a potentially powerful and active force. In this view, it is the attempts of dominant cultures to suppress pleasure that are viewed negatively, rather than the desire and drive of the masses to seek out pleasure and to subvert and resist the forces that try to oppress them. John Fiske (1987) has argued that just as in the nineteenth century travelling fairs were feared by the ruling classes as encouraging lewd and licentious behaviour in the populace, in the twentieth century it is television that has been demonised. In particular, Fiske talks about the way in which the specific pleasures offered by soap operas to their predominantly female audiences have been too readily dismissed and denigrated for producing precisely the kinds of embodied and emotional responses that defy control and moderation. More recently, reality television (see Chapter 7) has taken this to a new level, offering the viewer intimate insights into the emotional and physical realities of contestants' lives, celebrating excess and the breaking of all kinds of social niceties and taboos.

FROM WORK TO TEXT

Barthes distinguishes between work and **text** so as to place emphasis on the idea of narrative as process, something that cannot be contained, and is plural. Drawing on the original meaning of text as a kind of weaving, Barthes introduces the notion of intertextuality so as to escape the myth that the meanings of a text can be found in one origin or source. It is the work which is caught up in what Barthes calls the 'myth of filiation', where the author is the father figure and owner of the work. Again, Barthes relies on metaphors, referring to text as a kind of organism or network, where the distance between writing and reading is eroded and where readers play the text like a game or a musical instrument.

Barthes's theories have been particularly influential in helping to map the emergence of electronic literature, where the idea of a narrative as a bounded object becomes problematic. Barthes's idea of the text as something that is always in process is helpful for understanding how narratives might work on web pages for example, where the text is not something fixed or even stable, but is something which is constantly being 'refreshed'. Particularly with the emergence of hypertext fiction, and the idea of the text as something that is unique to every individual reading, Barthes's (1975b) concepts of the text and of the **'lexia'** as a unit of reading have been very influential.

WRITERLY AND PRODUCERLY TEXTS

In Barthes's (1975b) account of reading, a distinction is made between the 'scriptible' (writerly) and 'lisible' (readerly) text, where the former refers to avant-garde, experimental and self-conscious literary texts, and the latter to texts where the reader seemingly has to do very little work. At first glance this might seem to be a somewhat elitist stance, and one which is dismissive of the kind of easily digestible fiction we might find on the bestseller lists. However, Barthes is more concerned with the ways in which scriptible texts make demands of the reader and draw attention to their own textuality, rather than on their perceived quality or literary merit, and he does allow for the fact that lisible texts may in fact be turned into scriptible texts by the reader.

John Fiske (1987) has usefully extended Barthes's theory to account for what he calls 'producerly' texts in relation to television narratives. Taking as one of his examples the much castigated popular genre of the soap opera, Fiske argues that fans of these shows actively participate in the creation of meaning, for example, by writing in with suggestions for plot developments. Audiences also perform the role of writing or producing the text in their conversational interactions about the events and the characters that so enthrall them and sustain their attention across multiple episodes over seasons and years. Fiske also argues that television narratives regularly foreground their own textuality in a similar way to that described by Barthes, for example, with comic outtakes, 'the making of' programmes and shows dedicated to specific genres or retrospectives.

With the advent of the internet, we can see more and more opportunities for readers and viewers to become writers and producers, posting homemade videos on sites such as YouTube, or sharing fanfiction based on favourite literary or television characters on the many fansites and forums that now exist. Such technologies also make it possible for readers and audiences to pore over the minutiae of the making of these narratives and to share endless theories and hypotheses about authorial intention, symbols and signs embedded in the stories, and even plot holes and loose ends, whether intentional or accidental.

Barthes's focus on the reader must be understood in the context of his shift from the quasi-scientific focus of his earlier, classic structuralist work, towards the more pluralistic, open-ended and exploratory phase of his work which contributed so much to the development of poststructuralist theory. It must be remembered that nowhere does Barthes actually engage with real readers, and his concept of the reader is an abstraction conceived largely in opposition to the notion of the all-knowing author, and as part of his resistance to the idea of literary works as closed and consumable objects.

INTERTEXTUALITY

The notion of intertextuality has been particularly influential in the analysis of postmodern narratives, where parody and pastiche often feature prominently, and where the idea of fixed and stable meanings is constantly contested. However, John Fiske (1987) has argued that intertextuality is also important to understanding how contemporary television narratives work. He defines intertextuality as something that 'exists . . . in the space *between* texts' (108), arguing that unlike allusion, there is no need for the reader or viewer to be familiar with specific other reference points, so much as with the 'culture's image bank' (108) in which these meanings circulate. However, intertextuality also allows us to talk about different levels of response that a text may elicit. Thus when watching a film such as *Johnny English* (2003), viewers familiar with the James Bond franchise will pick up allusions to specific scenes, characters and visual and aural echoes, including the clothes worn by the hero, the locations and the soundtrack. Even if a viewer had never seen a Bond movie, according to Fiske he or she would readily be able to draw on the 'image bank' for the spy or secret agent, reimagined as it has been so many times across movies, tv shows, ads and so on.

Intertextuality relates closely to the idea of 'knowingness' in postmodern culture, and is a central feature of countless movies and tv shows from the 1990s, including the *Scream* movies, *The Simpsons* and *South Park*. Much humour and playfulness is derived from recycling and recirculating images and references from popular cultural texts, and from establishing a relationship with the viewer which is based on collusion and mutual understanding.

RECEPTION THEORY

The term **reception theory** is used to refer to the work of mainly European scholars concerned with how the reception of a work may change over time. Thus the idea that a text has a fixed meaning is replaced by the notion that the meaning of the work changes with each reading. While the focus of much of the analysis remains the (literary) text, this approach concerns itself with theories of meaning and interpretation, and with understanding reading as an ongoing process which offers each reader a unique experience. While many different strands of reception theory exist, and it may also be located in an umbrella category of 'reader response criticism', I shall focus here on the work of Wolfgang Iser, as his theories have been applied most consistently and most effectively to the reception of popular cultural and new media narratives.

GAP FILLING

Iser was influenced by the work of Roman Ingarden (1973), particularly his notion that literary texts have 'spots of indeterminacy' which the reader must fill or 'concretize' to give the text life. In this reconceptualisation of the literary work, it is neither completely identical with the text as created by the author, nor with the realisation of the text by the reader, but exists at a point of convergence between the two (Iser 2006). For Iser, indeed, the literary text is a kind of 'virtual reality' (58), and the job of the theorist is to try to account for how this virtual reality may be processed and understood. In Iser's own account of the development of his approach, 'the author's intention was replaced by the impact a piece of literature has on its potential recipient' and 'the focus switched from what the text means to what it does' (60).

Instead of Ingarden's 'spots of indeterminacy', Iser speaks of blanks or gaps that punctuate the text and which the reader has to negotiate in the 'act' of reading. Gaps or blanks in a literary text occur between paragraphs, chapters etc, and 'spur' or 'induce' the reader to seek for patterns and connections. The gaps or discontinuities trigger the reader's imagination and require the reader to *work* – not just to join the dots. Iser focused his analysis on the early novel, which was often published in instalments with multiple characters and interweaving plots. This emphasis on the particular characteristics and pleasures of serial forms helps explain why his theories have proved so influential, particularly as seriality has become so dominant in contemporary culture (see further Chapters 7 and 8).

Robert C. Allen (1992) draws heavily on Iser's work in setting out his own approach to 'audience-oriented criticism'. In particular, Allen argues that television soap operas rely on a process of **'gap filling'**, as audiences have to negotiate multiple plot lines, ad breaks, gaps between episodes, cliffhangers and so on, which necessitates not only retaining knowledge of what has already happened, but anticipating what may happen next, based on what they have already seen. This anticipation is part of the specific pleasure that **serial narratives** such as the soap opera offer, so that the pleasure of the text here is less about closure and resolution and more about endless disruption and deferral. Allen argues that Iser's claim that we can never experience a narrative in its totality is never more true than with the soap opera, whose plots extend over months and even years. He also speaks of the heightened enjoyment that the serial form can offer, and of the pleasure viewers derive from talking to each other in the gaps between episodes, reliving and replaying events, and deriving pleasure from the shared experience of viewing that particularly characterises the experience for die-hard, loyal fans.

Relying on the reader or viewer to work at producing a text's meanings can also be highly persuasive, for example, in the field of advertising where designer ads are often deliberately ambiguous or enigmatic, requiring the reader or viewer to work out just what product is actually being advertised. With new media technologies and social media, as we shall see in Chapter 8, audience involvement and interaction can be more instantaneous and can also be conducted on a much bigger scale.

THE IMPLIED READER

According to Iser (2006), the reader of a literary text adopts a 'wandering viewpoint' (65), negotiating numerous textual perspectives, including those of the characters, the narrator and the 'fictitious reader' as imagined by the text. The notion that texts imply a certain type of reader has been a controversial but nonetheless important contribution of Iser's. It's controversial because for some it carries with it connotations of an 'ideal' reader, while for others the fact that the **implied reader** is still a textual stance means it doesn't go far enough to bridge the gap with real readers. However, the concept is useful for highlighting the ways in which any teller of a story presupposes and assumes certain things about his or her audience, in terms of their knowledge base, attitudes, morals etc. For example, the implied reader of Charlotte Brontë's *Jane Eyre* (1847) is clearly expected to be familiar with the Bible and to have a working knowledge of French. The notion of the implied reader can also be useful for understanding the kind of relationship with the reader that the storyteller imagines, for example, whether he or she is addressed as a friend or is dealt with more distantly.

In Allen's application of Iser's theory to contemporary television, he notes that direct address is often a feature of television shows, where the host turns to the home audience and confides in them, shares his or her feelings etc. As Allen points out, this kind of cosy interaction was a familiar feature of the early novel, but by the beginning of the twentieth century the reader was much more likely to be largely ignored. In postmodern fiction, direct address and characterisation of the reader may be said to reappear. In *Slaughterhouse Five* (1987[1969]) by Kurt Vonnegut, the fictionalised version of the real-world author (discussed in Chapter 3) frequently intervenes in his own story to share jokes about his 'lousy little book' (9) or to chillingly reveal his involvement in the recounted events: 'That was I. That was me. That was the author of this book' (86).

Whereas the reader in fiction is usually only implied, on television audiences can be participants in the narrative, registering approval or disapproval (clapping, booing) and helping contestants or players in a quiz or game show by volunteering answers, as in the 'Ask the Audience' option on *Who Wants to Be a Millionaire?* (ITV UK, 1998–). Allen (1992) explains this performative role by reference to the wider social contract that television implies for its audience and demonstrates how viewers are recruited so as to be open to the advertisers' messages and are constantly reminded that '*you* are the "you" it wishes to speak to' (119).

Allen distinguishes between what he calls the rhetorical mode of address on television (where a face-to-face encounter is simulated) and the cinematic, where the viewer is only engaged covertly. The implicit reciprocity of television is therefore contrasted with the 'up front' economics of the cinema, where once you have paid for your ticket and sat through the ads, you expect to be left alone to enjoy the movie.

PREFERRED READINGS

As we saw in the last chapter, media and cultural studies often takes a bleak view of the role of ideology, positioning the reader or viewer as a passive consumer who has no control over the meanings and beliefs perpetuated by the mass media. In an attempt to address the seeming closing off of meanings these kinds of models imply, Stuart Hall's (1980) preferred reading theory brings into play the social situation and experience of the reader, while also recognising that some of the formal properties of media texts mean that some readings are preferred over others. Hall argued that readers or viewers whose position in society is closely aligned to that of the dominant ideology are much more likely to produce dominant or preferred readings. Readers or viewers occupying positions placing them in opposition to the dominant ideology, for example, ethnic minorities, gay or lesbian viewers, are more likely to produce oppositional readings. Most readers or viewers occupy a middle ground, producing negotiated readings of the text, generally conforming to the dominant ideology, but with some modifications or negotiations reflecting their specific situation.

Disney's *Frozen* (2014) has been widely celebrated for its refreshing new take on the 'princess' and seeming celebration of female empowerment. A negotiated reading of this movie would accept this preferred reading while also perhaps remaining critical of some aspects of the representation, for example, that the two main characters still conform to the notion of the princess in terms of their appearance or questioning some of the ways in which Elsa uses her magical powers. Oppositional readings to the film may readily be found online, for example, reading the film as a contemporary commentary on mental health, eating disorders or sexual preferences. As discussed more fully in Chapter 8, the internet has made it much easier for us to access and engage with different readings of a text, and has even made it possible for readers and audiences to create their own content where those readings become reimaginings of the story, for example, in fanfiction or fanvids.

Hall embraced the idea that texts could be polysemic, capable of sustaining multiple, even contradictory, meanings, but his theories were also influential in developing new understandings of audiences as potentially empowered, diverse and engaged participants in the production of a text's meanings. This is not to say that dominant ideologies have less influence, nor that all readings are necessarily equal, but the work of Hall and others was influential in demonstrating that reader and viewer engagement with texts is a rich and important area of study.

ACTIVE AND INTERACTIVE AUDIENCES

In his study of active audiences, John Fiske (1987) distinguishes between the powerless textual subject and the social subject, who 'has a history, lives in a particular social formation . . . and is constituted by a complex cultural history that is both social and textual' (62). His or her subjectivity results from '"real" social experience and from mediated or textual experience', and unlike the textual subject, his or her subjectivity extends beyond the moment of reading. As we shall see in the next chapter, focusing on the subjectivity of readers and audiences can be important in challenging dominant representations and the exclusion or marginalisation of others. In media and cultural studies in particular, the political dimension of audience and reception studies has long been understood, while in the field of narratology contextual approaches are beginning to incorporate and explore related questions and issues.

New technologies have facilitated closer analysis of the behaviour and responses of readers and audiences. David Morley's (1986) study of families watching tv together opened up fascinating insights into the power relations existing between family members in terms of their viewing, for example, who won the battle over the remote control. In the UK, the popular tv show *Gogglebox* (Channel 4, 2013–) allows viewers to observe other ordinary families watching familiar shows, while social media offers viewers another platform from which to observe what other viewers are thinking and feeling, and even to engage with characters and producers as the episodes are being broadcast.

ANALYSIS

In 2010, the UK telecommunications company BT brought to a climax a 'plot' campaign that had been running for around six years. The campaign featured the story of the ups and downs in the relationship of a young couple, Adam and Jane. The actor playing Adam, Kris Marshall, had already become a household name in the BBC sitcom *My Family* (2000–11), and the ad campaign offered a similarly modern take on the traditional family unit, with Jane a single mother who is older than Adam. The campaign followed a similar strategy to previous successes, notably the Nescafé Gold Blend and OXO ads from the 1980s and 1990s, developing ongoing plot lines and returning to familiar characters and situations, much in the vein of the soap opera. Gaps between the 'episodes' of the ad would therefore help to create and sustain active viewer engagement with the characters, as we followed their stories over a substantial period of time, seeing the children grow and the relationship develop.

The culmination of the campaign offered viewers caught up in the romance between the two characters the opportunity to participate in a poll determining the outcome of the relationship. On the BT website in 2010, the results of the poll were announced. The website directly addressed the viewer ('you') and constantly reinforced the idea that control for the story had been handed over to the viewer ('Here's how you voted'). BT tried to soften its corporate image by referring to itself as a 'family' expecting a 'new addition', but it also positioned itself as a company in touch with the 'nation' who are said to have responded in 'incredible' numbers. Meanwhile, the use of the present tense and exclamation mark for the dramatic header ('Jane is pregnant!') created the impression that the viewer is right in on the action, and also blurred the boundaries between the fictional and the real. However, the accompanying videos which appeared on the site, including outtakes from the ad, served to foreground its textuality, so performing the writerly or producerly function outlined by Barthes.

As technology has advanced, advertisers and corporations have experimented with interactive features, apps and augmented reality (discussed further in Chapter 8), to draw the viewer into the worlds they create and to engage the viewer in some kind of play rather than just try to sell them a message or product. However, even on BT's own 'Community Forums' it is evident that audiences and customers of the company didn't necessarily toe the BT line or subscribe to the preferred readings: for example, one contributor calls Jane 'a money grabbing witch', while another takes the discussion as an opportunity to complain about BT's services – 'Adam and Jane change to the BT browser and find it's as rubbish as we're finding it'.

CONCLUSION

The analysis of cultural texts has been dominated by a focus either on the intentions of the writer/producer or on meaning as somehow being contained within the text, simply waiting for the reader to come along and extract or decode that meaning. Focusing on the role of the reader as ongoing practice and active engagement liberates all concerned: authorial intentions and textual meaning are no longer seen as fixed or immutable, while readers come out of the shadows to be identified as flesh and blood, historically situated beings capable of unexpected, powerful and creative responses that keep the narrative alive. As we shall see in Chapter 8, new media narratives have been said to extend the possibilities for reader involvement and participation even further, making a focus on the role of readers and audiences ever more pertinent and timely.

SUGGESTED READING

Barthes's essays have been widely anthologised (most notably in *Image-Music-Text*), and many are now available online. John Fiske's *Television Culture* applies many of Barthes's terms and concepts to television, and Robert Allen's chapter 'Audience-Oriented Criticism' provides an excellent account of Iser's theories in relation to television soap operas. Barthes's work has been particularly influential for the study of electronic literature and new media narratives, including Landow's *Hypertext 3.0*. Meanwhile, Marie-Laure Ryan's works, including *Narrative as Virtual Reality*, refer extensively to both Barthes and Iser, and I have drawn on Iser's work to explore emerging new forms such as Twitterfiction (discussed more fully in Chapter 8). Elizabeth Freund's *The Return of the Reader* locates the work of Iser within a wider tradition of work concerned with the role of readers in literary texts. Most media textbooks will carry sections on audiences, and audience studies has emerged as a distinctive subdiscipline within this context.

REFERENCES

Allen, R.C. (1992) Audience-Oriented Criticism and Television. In *Channels of Discourse: Reassembled*, ed. R.C. Allen. London: Routledge, 101–37.

Barthes, R. (1975a) *The Pleasure of the Text*. Transl. R. Miller. New York: Hill and Wang.

Barthes, R. (1975b) *S/Z*. Transl. R. Miller. London: Jonathan Cape.

Barthes, R. (1977) *Image-Music-Text*. Transl. S. Heath. London: Harper Collins. [Includes 'The Death of the Author' and 'From Work to Text'.]

Fiske, J. (1987) *Television Culture*. London: Routledge.

Freund, E. (1987) *The Return of the Reader: Reader-Response Criticism*. London: Methuen.

Hall, S. (1980) Encoding/Decoding. In *Culture, Media and Language*, eds. S. Hall, D. Hobson, A. Lowe and P. Willis. London: Hutchinson, 128–39.

Ingarden, R. (1973) *The Cognition of the Literary Work of Art*. Transl. R.A. Crowly and K.R. Olsen. Evanston: Northwestern University Press.

Iser, W. (1974) *The Implied Reader*. Baltimore: Johns Hopkins University Press.

Iser, W. (1978) *The Act of Reading*. Baltimore: Johns Hopkins University Press.

Iser, W. (2006) *How to Do Theory*. Oxford: Blackwell.

Landow, G. (2006) (3rd ed.) *Hypertext 3.0*. Baltimore: Johns Hopkins University Press.

Morley, D. (1986) *Family Television*. London: Comedia.

Ryan, M-L. (2001) *Narrative as Virtual Reality: Immersion and Interactivity in Literature and Electronic Media*. Baltimore: Johns Hopkins University Press.

Thomas, B. (2014) 140 Characters in Search of a Story: Twitterfiction as an Emerging Narrative Form. In *Analysing Digital Fiction*, eds. A. Bell, A. Ensslin and H. Rustad. London: Routledge, 94–108.

Vonnegut, K. (1987[1969]) *Slaughterhouse Five*. London: Triad Grafton.

6

'GENDER TROUBLE'

FEMINIST APPROACHES TO NARRATIVE

'By sharing your story you're showing that the world that sexism *does* exist, it *is* faced by women *everyday* and it *is* a valid problem to discuss.'
(www.everydaysexism.com)

'Gender is produced *through* narrative processes, not prior to them.'
(Robinson 1991: 198)

According to Susan Lanser (1991), feminism and narratology 'cannot really be said to have a history' other than a 'few gestures of synthesis' (610), while Robyn Warhol (1999) has claimed that 'Ten years ago, a feminist had to feel guilty about being a narratologist' (342). Nevertheless, we have seen in earlier chapters that contemporary narratology does concern itself increasingly with identifying and challenging dominant ideologies and with contextualising discussions of technique and form. For feminist narratologists this means primarily a focus on patriarchy and the marginalisation of women in contemporary narratives – a 'gender-conscious' narratology which addresses head on the neglect of **gender** in many previous studies and approaches. Such an approach also queries the assumption that models that focus mainly on texts written and produced by men can in any way be claimed to be universal. Feminist narratology is also distinctive in its emphasis on the importance of the reception of narratives, locating readers and viewers as historically situated and allowing space for the consideration of affective and subjective responses.

Feminist narratology draws on theories and approaches to gender from literary criticism and media and film studies rather than on developing models or theoretical terms to counter those developed by male theorists (Page 2007). However, Warhol (1999) claims it is still distinctive in its approach, combining as it does close textual analysis with situating texts in specific contexts. Narratological approaches also provide more of an emphasis on the underlying structures of a narrative, moving beyond the tendency in much feminist criticism to focus purely on the representation of individual characters and the extent to which they are being stereotyped. Feminist narratologists interrogate terms such as gender, sex and sexuality, with the emergence of 'queer narratology' in particular addressing the latter. As a result, the focus is on 'gender not as a predetermined condition of the production of texts, but as a textual effect' (Warhol 1999: 343). Many introductions to narrative do not even mention gender or feminism, suggesting that perhaps we still have some way to go in detaching contemporary narratology from the formalist and universalising tendencies with which it has been associated.

In this chapter I will give an overview of some of the issues facing feminism today, as well as outlining some of the key theories and approaches that have been developed to address the ways in which women have been (mis)represented in contemporary narratives. I will then return to consider how feminist narratology locates itself in relation to these traditions, and the extent to which it offers a distinctive approach or methodology.

CONTEMPORARY FEMINISMS

Second-wave feminist criticism from the 1970s and 1980s focused on highlighting inequalities and exposing the marginalisation or 'symbolic annihilation' (Tuchmann 1978) of women in literature and the media. However, while feminist theorists may have shared certain fundamental beliefs, divisions in approach and philosophy have resulted in the term feminism being increasingly contested. In particular, the dominance of early feminist theory by white Western intellectuals has been criticised for excluding considerations of ethnicity, sexuality and age. More recently, 'postfeminism' raises the question of whether or not feminism as a politicised movement about and for women is even relevant in an age when equality seems to have been achieved, in most Western industrialised nations at least, and where strong role models appear to be in abundance in the media. However, at the turn of the twenty-first century, feminism seems to be enjoying something of a resurgence, especially on university campuses in the UK and the US and online, with the emergence of 'digital feminism' and campaigns taking place via social media, which aim to expose and fight against sexism.

Online feminist activists have focused on highlighting gender inequality in the news (Who Makes the News; www.whomakesthe news.org) and exposing stereotyping in the media and film industries (The Representation Project; www.therepresentationproject.org). On social media the hashtag #notbuyingit has been used to expose sexist advertising campaigns and to encourage women to boycott the companies behind them. Such work is useful in helping to highlight continuing inequalities in the ways women are portrayed in the media, for example, taking supporting rather than central roles or being given prominence only if they conform to the media's notion of what is considered attractive or 'sexy'.

FEMINIST STUDIES ACROSS MEDIA

Feminist narratology to date has most consistently drawn on feminist studies from the field of literature. Concerned with the politics of representation, work in this area often focuses on understanding why female authors or genres associated with women have been neglected or marginalised. Feminist criticism has challenged the idea of the male dominated literary canon (e.g. Showalter 1977) and argued that women's writing needs to be evaluated according to different sets of criteria, and in its own specific terms. Feminist criticism has also focused on specific aspects of narrative such as characterisation and plot, for example, examining the dominance of the 'marriage plot' in the classic realist novel and tracing its persistence in contemporary genres such as 'chick lit' or the romantic comedy (Warhol 2010). Critics have also examined how gender informs our responses to narrative voice, for example, whether we assume an unnamed narrator is male or female and how we as readers are positioned in terms of gender, as in the branding and marketing of stories aimed at girls or boys.

In film studies, Laura Mulvey's (1975) theory of the male gaze demonstrated how widespread the objectification of women is in mainstream Hollywood movies and how women continue to be marginalised behind as well as in front of the camera. Mulvey's theory has been influential in analysing how women are depicted in television and advertising narratives, though it has also been criticised for seemingly assuming that the male gaze is always a heterosexual one and that women are incapable of being desiring subjects taking visual pleasure from the 'female gaze' (Gamman and Marshmant 1988).

Gender has been a major focus of studies of contemporary advertising perhaps because the industry has a reputation for objectifying the female body and for perpetuating the idea that men and women occupy completely separate spheres. As John Berger (1990[1972]: 47) puts it, from classical art through to contemporary ads, the convention is that 'Men act and women appear'. Advertising clearly targets audiences in terms of gender: in the commercial breaks punctuating football matches ads for beer, DIY products and the like reinforce the idea that this is a male preserve. Ads for the same product also target men and women differently. For example, in a concurrent campaign for Clinique 'Happy', the male figure in the ad for the fragrance 'For Men' appears alone and carefree, doing some kind of dance. In the ad targeted towards women, the female model is depicted in a maternal role, swaddling a young baby. More recent ads for the fragrance have featured men and women together, but they still perpetuate the idea of separate spheres with the men pictured as sportsmen or rock stars and the women in supporting roles, dressed as cheerleaders, or a homemaker proffering a celebratory cake.

Many ads perpetuate the notion that the 'natural' place for women is in the home: where men are shown taking on domestic chores they are inept or childlike. Women are also routinely objectified, posed so as to appeal to the male gaze, or reduced to a set of body parts, with the image cropped so as to focus on the mouth, the legs or the breasts of the model. Goffman's (1979) *Gender Advertisements* remains a key text for identifying the 'ritual poses' employed by advertisers and the ways in which these help to reinforce gender stereotypes.

Gender has also been a contentious point of discussion when it comes to videogames. A male-dominated industry, it has appeared as though women have been sidelined not just as characters and actors within the games, but also as players. In her study of the language of gaming, Ensslin (2012) argues that to meet the assumed needs of their audience, two types of female characters have been dominant: the damsel in distress and the femme fatale. Female avatars are often hypersexualised and objectified, and female characters tend to be 'backgrounded' (Masso, 2009, 2011, cited by Ensslin). Ensslin discusses competing interpretations of the Lara Croft character from cyberfeminists who see her as a new icon, to those who dismiss her as a 'cyberbimbo'. However, along with what many critics have seen as the increased importance of narrative in recent high-profile games, it does appear as though game designers and writers are trying to provide more rounded and central roles for women, for example, with the character of Ellie in *The Last of Us*, a partner to the main male character rather than a burden and a 'spirited and foul-mouthed heroine' according to Farokhmanesh (2014). At the same time, many games remain intrinsically normative when it comes to gender, forcing players to choose between male or female characters with very different attributes, powers and skills.

ESSENTIALISM AND ANTIESSENTIALISM

Across media, it is undoubtedly the 'images of women' approach that has dominated feminist criticism to date, picking out female characters for condemnation or praise and tracing common patterns and types of representation across time. At worst, this approach can result in reinforcing the notion of women as victims or in a rather naïve categorisation of representations into positive and negative. It can also help to perpetuate the notion that men and women are essentially different, and that merely helping to highlight and celebrate female qualities and values is somehow sufficient to challenge the domination of the male.

With poststructuralist feminist approaches, this kind of essentialising is replaced with a more radical and searching critique of gender not as a category so much as a way of actively constructing subjects as masculine and feminine. Here the category of 'woman' is not seen as mapping onto a preexisting identity to be revealed by a more accurate or truthful representation (Butler 1999). Instead, 'gender trouble' constantly destabilises and unsettles the very notion of a commonly shared gender identity or the notion that a person 'has' a gender. Any kind of universalizing or totalizing is thus rejected, and the language by which we theorise gender is to be constantly interrogated.

Alongside Butler, it is the so-called French feminists who have had the most profound impact on contemporary theory. Extending and critiquing the idea of binary oppositions from classical structuralism (see Chapter 2), Cixous (2000[1975]: 265) argues that woman is 'always on the side of passivity' whether the particular opposition is father/mother, head/heart or sun/moon, resulting in a perpetual privileging of the masculine. Influenced by poststructuralism and psychoanalysis, French feminists view subjectivity as a process, not as something which is given beforehand or fixed. In their radical critique of the phallocentrism of language, a whole new way of writing ('écriture féminine') is proposed, transgressing existing norms to explore a kind of language that defies logic and embraces looseness and ambiguity.

The critique of language is not new in itself: in the early part of the twentieth century Virginia Woolf (1929) noted that women writers were constrained by having to write 'a man's sentence' (73) and by the 'arcades or domes' into which these sentences are combined, 'made by men out of their own needs for their own uses' (73–4). Woolf also argues that women's books need to be interruptible and 'adapted to the body' (74). In this respect, Woolf seems to anticipate the work of the French feminists in their focus on reading and writing as embodied activities, although in the case of écriture feminine these practices are importantly not just the domain of women.

GENDERED TELEVISION

Television's place in the home and its centrality to the domestic routines that traditionally centre around the mother has made it a major focus of study for feminists. For example, echoing Woolf's essay, Tania Modleski (1983) has argued that the episodic structure of soap operas accommodates women's need to be 'interruptible', allowing for distraction to be pleasurable, and also drawing on women's socialised skills in attending to the needs of others.

Content analysis has been used widely in television studies to identify the dominant 'images of women' at play. Diana Meehan's (1983) typology of women characters on prime time US television from the 1950s to the 1980s showed that women tended to be placed in roles subordinate to those of men, very rarely being allowed to display any autonomy. Though the recurring categories that Meehan found, including the imp, the bitch, the matriarch, the decoy and the siren, related to tv shows aired decades ago, they are still readily identifiable in today's narratives. Even where women are shown in authoritative roles, or as successful in professional careers, this is often at the expense of their personal lives. For example, in the groundbreaking UK detective series *Prime Suspect*, the main character, DI Jane Tennyson, is shown as tough and uncompromising in the workplace, but when she returns home her loneliness and insecurities come to the fore. As well as showing strong women to be vulnerable, television narratives also frequently show women being punished for stepping out of line or taking on 'masculine' roles, whether that is by portraying as them as unhappy or dissatisfied or showing them being physically attacked or victimised in some way.

In *Television Culture*, John Fiske (1987) goes beyond observing images of women or the narrative structures of contemporary narratives to explore the ways in which 'television copes with, and helps to produce, a crucial categorization of its viewers into masculine and feminine subjects' (179), using the soap opera as an example of a 'feminine narrative' and the action adventure series or crime drama as typifying the 'masculine'. Fiske argues that the soap opera's 'infinitely extended middle' (180) offers an alternative to the beginning, middle and end structure of traditional realist narratives, resisting closure and the restoring of equilibrium. Instead, the world of the soap is one of 'perpetual disturbance and threat' (180), with viewers taking pleasure in the transgression of societal norms and conventions. The mini-climaxes which this kind of narrative offers allows for the 'articulation of a specific feminine definition of desire and pleasure' (181), with the emphasis on process not product, on pleasure as ongoing and cyclical, not climactic and final. The multiplicity of characters and plotlines in soaps are 'impossible for the narrative structure to control' (194), so that the reader is 'never allowed a stable reading position' (194–5), as so many different perspectives on events are offered. Fiske celebrates the decentredness and denial of a unified reading position that this kind of narrative entails, seeing this as a potentially 'masculine-free zone' which 'whittles away at patriarchy's power' (197) through its constant interrogation of patriarchy and its legitimation of feminine values.

Masculine narratives are less polysemic, and are structured to produce 'greater narrative and ideological closure' (198), allowing male viewers to come to terms with the differences between their experiences and the ideological construction of masculinity. In shows such as *The A-Team*, Fiske argues, masculinity is a performance, with each episode bound to end in success, and personal relationships, particularly with other men, being externalised onto some kind of goal, with clear hierarchies and leaders, and only very minimal dialogue.

Fiske is at pains to deny that the distinction he draws between masculine and feminine narratives in any way indicates essential differences between men and women: instead it is 'a product of the politics and practices of the family in capitalism' (218) and is less about their different textual conventions than the 'reading relations' they invite. Since Fiske's study was published, it could be argued that the differences in these 'textual conventions' have diminished. It has even been argued that television as a whole has become more and more 'feminized' (Ball 2012), with the emergence of ensemble dramas featuring predominantly female casts (*Girls, Desperate Housewives, Orange is the New Black*), and with television genres traditionally associated with daytime television, for example, cookery shows or 'lifestyle' television, starting to dominate the prime-time schedules.

At the same time, the emergence of the 'multistrand' narrative form characteristic of shows like *Lost* has seen serial narratives become much more dominant, with their large casts, complex interweaving plots and multiple perspectives keeping audiences guessing, and also serving to prolong and disperse the pleasures of the text. Indeed, Christine Geraghty (cited by Jeffries 2013), an expert on television soap operas, has bemoaned the fact that HBO shows such as *The Wire* or AMC's *Mad Men* have been lauded for their innovative plots when she claims that soaps have been using similar techniques for decades. Similarly, Geraghty and others have been critical of the ways in which soaps, especially in the UK, seem to have abandoned their traditional, largely female audience, employing storylines based on crime, violence and large-scale disasters instead of slow-moving plots in which dialogue and personal relations are to the fore.

NARRATIVE DESIRE AND AFFECT

Soap operas have received a great deal of attention not just because of their narrative structure, but also because of the 'reading relations' they invite, and the ways in which these seems to offer an alternative to, even a subversion of, dominant patriarchal ideologies. Drawing on psychoanalytical theory, Tania Modleski's (1983) study of US soaps argues that a relationship of 'nearness', akin to that of the mother–daughter bond, characterises how the soap viewer relates to the fictional characters in the show. Traditionally, overidentification with characters is frowned upon, but feminist critics often set out to challenge these assumptions and the marginalisation of what may have been outlawed or dispreferred in terms of accepted readings or audience responses.

Feminist narratologists have contested attempts to categorise or define female sexuality in simplistic terms, for example, by reading the constant deferral of climax in the soap opera as somehow reflective of the female orgasm. Instead, they argue that the kinds of pleasures identified are 'not intrinsic to female bodies' but reflect a process which 'structures this model of pleasure into the feminine subjects who repeatedly rehearse it' (Warhol 1999: 353–4). In *Loving with a Vengeance* (1982), Modleski explores how female desire has been represented in film as either impossible or dangerous and duplicitous, but finds that female readers' responses to mass-produced fantasies on film and television are much more complex and contradictory than had previously been allowed.

Feminist critics may therefore concern themselves with reclaiming genres that have been neglected or dismissed in the past, for example, the melodrama, as a means of exploring what kinds of problems and tensions in women's lives these genres may address. In her book *Having a Good Cry* (2003), Robyn Warhol explores the 'effeminate feelings' that dominant ideology tries to suppress or marginalise. As well as opening up narratology to the study of affective responses of narrative texts, Warhol's work has also led to more attention being paid to popular cultural forms. Warhol (1999) writes about her 'guilty cravings' for 'feminine' emotional excess (341), particularly with regards to the daytime soap, arguing that the genre 'puts its viewers through the paces of *feeling* femininity' (348). Warhol draws on the tried-and-tested method of close reading as a means to articulate and foreground the experience of being a long-standing fan of a soap, and of her desires as a reader. But for Warhol, reading 'always happens in and to a body' (ix) connecting her work, and feminist narratology more broadly, with important ongoing debates within feminism about the tensions between women's lived experiences of the body and the cultural meanings that are attached to their bodies as represented by others.

A WEB OF OUR OWN

Donna Haraway's 'A Cyborg Manifesto' (1991) held out the possibility of a 'postgender world', celebrating the World Wide Web as a potential space for liberating women from the historical forms of domination through which they have been oppressed. As well as providing a forum for feminist activism, the World Wide Web may also be said to provide more opportunities for women to tell their stories in their own words and to play with gender identities and sexuality. Web-based forums and social media also provide researchers with rich material when it comes to analysing the responses of audiences and readers. Women are said to be the most prolific of writers of web-based fanfiction, a genre whereby already existing characters and storyworlds provide a platform for creativity, invention and play, often resulting in subversive reinterpretations of the source texts. Famously, the phenomenal success of E.L. James's *Fifty Shades of Grey* (2011) is said to have originated with the author's experiments in writing Twilight-based fanfic. James's success has also reignited debates about female sexuality, and reflects the fact that a lot of fanfiction written by women is highly erotic in content, often challenging taboos and subverting heteronormative discourses, particularly in the subgenre of fanfic known as slash.

The phenomenon of self-publishing offers writers the opportunity to bypass traditional routes to getting a work published, and the internet has been hailed by many for its democratising potential. But certainly the proliferation of narrative forms that we find online raises new and important questions regarding voice and also offers us the potential for exploring in much more depth than has previously been possible what readers and audiences do, and also what they feel, when they discover new stories, new characters and new worlds.

ANALYSIS

My approach in what follows draws on Robyn Warhol's (1999) attempt to rebrand narratology's focus on close reading as a method for examining the role 'formal properties and operations . . . play in structuring the very audience response we seek to study' (346). I also try to resist the temptation to simply categorise representations as positive or negative, reflecting what Ruth Page (2007) sees as an 'increasing interest in narratives where the correlations between gender, sex and sexuality are exposed as fluid, multiple, and socially constructed' (192–3).

The US tv show *Sex and the City* (1998–2004) is often hailed as a watershed moment in the discussion of the representation of women in popular culture. It is also seen as a key text for any discussion of the notion of postfeminism. In its focus on a group of single career-minded New Yorkers, *Sex and the City* seemed to offer viewers empowered female characters who spoke about sex, marriage and other women in uncompromising terms which many found shocking and unsettling, but also exhilarating. However, the series has prompted ongoing debate about the extent to which the show's aims or message could in any way be described as feminist. Many critics bemoaned the reliance on the traditional marriage plot in Carrie's relationship with 'Mr Big', and the fact that all of the lead women conformed to the conventional Hollywood glamour image, never actually being seen to 'work' at the careers they seemingly were so successful at, jarred with many.

Sex and the City presents the viewer with clear character types or archetypes and forms of behaviour which arguably help to reinscribe dominant versions of femininity. Despite the seeming success of the central characters, each is at various points depicted as having to sacrifice personal happiness for career success, and despite the seeming freedoms they enjoy, often this appears to incur some kind of emotional cost. To some extent, therefore, the show seems to conform to the pattern identified by Meehan from her study of US prime-time tv from decades earlier.

The format of the show is close to that of the situation comedy, providing a 'problem of the week' usually focused on one of the central characters, which is then resolved within the episode, returning the characters to the familiar and reassuring status quo of the 'situation' that defines the drama. The show features the voice-over of the main character, Carrie Bradshaw, framing the narrative with a question about relationships, monogamy etc, followed by some kind of reflection on the events of that episode as they unfolded. Carrie's voice-over often betrays her insecurities and fragility as a character. For some critics, this is a refreshing alternative to the moralistic tone of male voice-overs on tv, while others see the focus on her insecurities and inability always to reach conclusions as disempowering and conforming to gender stereotypes.

The show's focus on the dilemmas facing women in contemporary society may sometimes appear to be simplistically presented and narrowly defined, for example, whether or not to date younger men ('Valley of the Twenty-Something Guys') or men who suffer from premature ejaculation ('Shortcomings'). Nevertheless, the show may be said to be uncompromising in showing the characters (both male and female) wrestling with their gendered identities and expressing their frustration with the limits these impose on them.

Since *Sex and the City*, tv shows such as *Girls* (2012–) and movies such as *Bridesmaids* (2011) have drawn on the successful formula of the female ensemble piece, heavy on irony and female-oriented storylines. *Girls* positions itself as a more grittily realistic version of *Sex and the City*, with lots of bad sex and a lead character, Hannah, who has complexes and issues with her appearance and size. While Sarah Jessica Parker remained distinct from author Candace Bushnell, who was the inspiration for *Sex and the City*, interviews with Lena Dunham, who plays Hannah in *Girls*, often draw on the similarities between the actress and her onscreen role. In addition, while movies based on *Sex and the City* were released, the extratextual reach of *Girls*, taking in Pinterest, Tumblr and Facebook pages, testifies to the fact that the show has struck a chord with its audience, and that that audience wants to continue exploring the issues it raises long after the episodes have aired.

Bridesmaids likewise celebrates female friendship, and offers a female version of the successful 'gross out' US comedies, such as *Knocked Up*. For some, simply reversing the gender of the lead characters does not really offer progress, and the film also seems to have at its centre quite a conventional marriage plot in which the main character overcomes all obstacles and eventually finds her Prince

Charming. Nevertheless, the use of humour has proved very effective, and goes some way at least to challenge the stereotype that feminists can't do comedy.

Attracting a slightly younger audience, *The Hunger Games* trilogy has been claimed by some to offer a positive role model for young girls in the character of Katniss Everdeen. Following the success of the novels, two film adaptations have been released to date, and there have been numerous online extensions to the franchise, including various social media accounts and an interactive website. Some of this content might be said to reinforce gender stereotypes, for example, the fashion-based 'Capitol Couture' campaign accompanying the release of the second movie in the franchise. But it soon becomes apparent that this is part of the same scathing satire of the contemporary obsession with celebrity and staging 'reality' that we see in the books and the film, with Katniss leading the fight against the 'system' which relies on these means to suppress the populace.

The film adaptation of *Catching Fire* (2013) opens with Katniss wielding her weapon while her companion looks on, and it is she who seemingly plays with the emotions of others, using her relationship with Peeta as a ploy and keeping the audience guessing throughout about her intentions and her true feelings. Though some have argued that Katniss's main strength is traditionally female, as she uses her ability to form relationships with others to her advantage, and also that she remains an object of desire for others (Taber, Woloshyn and Lane 2013), Katniss's focus throughout remains on challenging the system, even if this means sacrificing her own feelings and those of the people closest to her. Katniss grows up in a female environment and relies on her own skills and physical strength to become the ultimate competitor. Katniss's journey seems to correspond closely to that set out by Propp, Campbell and others for the folkloric hero, while Peeta is portrayed as vulnerable, both physically and emotionally. Thus while some argue that this structure entails a kind of heteronormativity that is restricting (Taber, Woloshyn and Lane 2013), they acknowledge that the trilogy does raise important issues and that 'readers must continue to problematise gendered representations' (158) rather than rely on simplistic notions of what makes a 'strong' male or female character.

CONCLUSION

Although much of this chapter has been concerned with the term feminism and how its politics, methods and approach have influenced the study of narrative, the extent to which the term galvanises or alienates people continues to be a matter of heated debate. Less contentious is the idea that 'the underrepresentation of women in positions of power and influence' (The Representation Project; www.therepresentationproject.org) continues to be something which we need to address. Nevertheless, many of these contemporary campaigns reject a narrow focus on gender, instead considering the situation of women alongside that of other marginalised groups in society. Similarly, while women interested in studying issues of gender and sexuality would perhaps have been steered towards courses in 'Women's Studies' in the 1980s and 1990s, now courses on 'Gender and Sexuality' offer a wider focus, negotiating often controversial points of intersection and division between communities, including gay and lesbian activists, or those campaigning for intersex and transgender individuals. The term 'queer narratology' has emerged in recent years referring to a body of work (Roof 1996; Warhol and Lanser forthcoming) that responds to the rise of 'queer theory' in literary, media and cultural studies since the 1990s, exploring representations of gay and lesbian characters, but also asking whether the heteronormativity of narrative itself needs to be 'queered'.

FOLLOW-UP ACTIVITIES

1. Reimagine a narrative by 'flipping' the gender of the protagonist. For example, you could rewrite an extract from a novel narrated by a boy or man (e.g. *The Catcher in the Rye*) with a female protagonist or explore how a female version of James Bond or Doctor Who might work.

2. Using a tv schedule as your starting point, discuss whether it is still possible to categorise the shows into masculine and feminine narratives in the way that Fiske suggests.

3. Apply Meehan's (1983) categories for female character types to a current tv show.

4. Compare the ad breaks during a screening of an action adventure film or tv show with those that accompany a romantic comedy or soap opera. What does this tell us about the expected audiences for these types of narratives?

SUGGESTED READING

Robyn Warhol's essay 'Guilty Cravings' and her book *Having a Good Cry* both offer interesting insights into feminist issues in relation to popular cultural forms such as the soap opera. Ruth Page's chapter 'Gender' and her book *Literary and Linguistic Approaches to Feminist Narratology* both provide comprehensive and clear accounts of the emergence of feminist approaches within the context of postclassical narratologies.

Laura Mulvey's essay on the male gaze remains highly influential, while John Berger's treatment of the same subject in *Ways of Seeing* extends the discussion to visual art and to advertising.

For an excellent discussion of feminist theory in relation to television narratives, including discussion of Meehan and Modleski, French feminism and Judith Butler, see Kaplan's chapter 'Feminist Criticism and Television'. A comprehensive range of essays on a variety of narrative forms is also provided in *The Gender and Media Reader*.

Robyn Warhol and Susan Lanser's forthcoming volume of essays promises to provide a 'diverse spectrum of queer and feminist challenges to the theory and interpretation of narrative'. Meanwhile, a good introduction to some key texts is provided by the online 'living handbook of narratology' (www.lhn.uni-hamburg.de/article/gender-and-narrative).

REFERENCES

Ball, V. (2012) The "FEMINIZATION" of British Television and the Re-Traditionalization of Gender, *Feminist Media Studies*, 12(2), 248–64.

Berger, J. (1990[1972]) *Ways of Seeing*. Harmondsworth: Penguin.

Butler, J. (1999) (2nd ed.) *Gender Trouble*. London: Routledge.

Cixous, H. (2000[1975]) Sorties. In *Modern Criticism and Theory: A Reader*, eds. D. Lodge and N. Wood. Harlow: Longman, 358–65.

Ensslin, A. (2012) *The Language of Gaming*. Basingstoke: Palgrave.

Farokhmanesh, M. (2014) How Naughty Dog Created a Partner not a Burden, with Ellie in *The Last of Us*. Accessed 20/3/15 at http://www.polygon.com/2014/3/22/5531146/the-last-of-us-ellie-was-designed-to

Fiske, J. (1987) *Television Culture*. London: Routledge.

Gamman, L. and Marshmant, M. (eds.) (1988) *The Female Gaze*. London: Women's Press.

Goffman, E. (1979) *Gender Advertisements*. New York: Harper & Row.

Haraway, D.J. (1991) *Simians, Cyborgs and Women: The Reinvention of Nature*. New York: Routledge.

Jeffries, S. (2013) Soap Operas: Has the Bubble Burst? Accessed 20/3/15 at http://www.theguardian.com/tv-and-radio/2013/oct/01/soap-operas-has-the-bubble-burst

Kaplan, E.A. (1992) Feminist Criticism and Television. In *Channels of Discourse: Reassembled*, ed. R.C. Allen. London: Routledge, 247–83.

Kearney, M.C. (ed.) (2012) *The Gender and Media Reader*. London: Routledge.

Lanser, S. (1991) Toward a Feminist Narratology. In *Feminisms: An Anthology*, eds. R. Warhol and D.P. Herndl. New Brunswick: Rutgers University Press, 610–29.

Meehan, D. (1983) *Ladies of the Evening: Women Characters of Prime-Time Television*. Metuchen, NJ: Scarecrow Press.

Modleski, T. (1982) *Loving with a Vengeance: Mass-Produced Fantasies for Women*. Hamden, CT: Archon.

Modleski, T. (1983) The Rhythms of Reception: Daytime Television and Women's Work. In *Regarding Television: Critical Approaches – an Anthology*, ed. E.A. Kaplan. Frederick, MD: University Publications of America.

Mulvey, L. (1975) Visual Pleasure and Narrative Cinema. *Screen*, 16(3), 6–18.

Page, R. (2006) *Literary and Linguistic Approaches to Feminist Narratology*. Basingstoke: Palgrave.

Page, R. (2007) Gender. In *The Cambridge Companion to Narrative*, ed. D. Herman. Cambridge: Cambridge University Press, 189–202.

Robinson, S. (1991) *Engendering the Subject: Gender and Self-Representation in Contemporary Women's Fiction*. New York: State University of New York Press.

Roof, J. (1996) *Come as You Are: Sexuality and Narrative*. New York: Columbia University Press.

Showalter, E. (1977) *A Literature of Their Own: British Women Novelists from Brontë to Lessing*. Princeton: Princeton University Press.

Spender, D. (1985) *Man Made Language*. London: Routledge & Kegan Paul.

Taber, N., Woloshyn, V. and Lane, L. (2013) 'She's MORE LIKE a GUY' and 'HE'S MORE LIKE a TEDDY BEAR': GIRLS' PERCEPTION of VIOLENCE and GENDER in *The Hunger Games. Journal of Youth Studies*, 16(8), 1022–37.

Tuchman, G. (1978) The SYMBOLIC ANNIHILATION of WOMEN by the MASS MEDIA. In *Hearth and Home: Images of Women in the Mass Media*, eds. G. Tuchman, A.K. Daniels and J. Benet. New York: Oxford University Press, 3–45.

Warhol, R. (1999) Guilty Cravings: What Feminist Narratology Can Do for Cultural Studies. In *Narratologies: New Perspectives on Narrative Analysis*, ed. D. Herman. Columbus: Ohio State University Press, 340–55.

Warhol, R. (2003) *Having a Good Cry: Effeminate Feelings and Pop-Cultural Forms*. Columbus: Ohio State University Press.

Warhol, R. (2010) Gender. In *Teaching Narrative Theory*, eds. D. Herman, B. McHale and J. Phelan. New York: The Modern Language Association of America, 237–51.

Warhol, R. and Lanser, S. (forthcoming) *Narrative Theory Unbound: Queer and Feminist Interventions*. Columbus: Ohio State University Press.

Woolf, V. (1977[1929]) *A Room of One's Own*. London: Grafton Books.

7

NARRATIVE AND GENRE

'There is no genreless text.'

(Derrida 1990[1980]: 61)

WHY STUDY GENRE?

Genre, from the French meaning 'type' or 'kind', is a way of classify-
ing phenomena based on shared properties or qualities. With regard
to narrative, the attempt to categorise ways of telling stories may be
traced back to classical antiquity and persists into the present day:
in most stores books, music and videogames are arranged by genre,
while television schedules have clearly defined time slots for certain
types of programming. A focus on genre means going beyond the
confines of the individual text, allowing us to identify patterns and
relations existing across texts and across media platforms. It can also
help to provide a historical context for narrative and demonstrate
how texts are used by readers, including the social impact they may
have in both reflecting and shaping cultural norms and values.

Resistance to classification and fixed categories has arguably always
existed in the form of parody or pastiche. However, subverting, unsettling and blurring genre boundaries has come to be a key characteristic
of the postmodern, self-consciously foregrounding and playing with
genre conventions to produce complex, hybrid new forms that often

defy definition and that blur the boundaries between fact and fiction. At the same time, genre theory has moved beyond formalistic classification to understand the social function of genres and the role played by readers and audiences in ensuring their relevance and popularity.

In the field of literature, 'genre fiction' is often used as a pejorative term, with the distinction between this kind of writing and the literary classics being constantly upheld and redefined by bookshops, publishers, literary prizes and so on. As a result, discussion of genre is often absent from narrative studies, focusing as it does largely on canonical literary texts. In film studies, too, genre has been perceived as something which stifles creativity, limiting the free play of meanings (Altman 1984). Studies of genre in film are perceived negatively as focusing only on texts that have parallels in literature (Neale 2008) and are associated with the worst excesses of structuralism and formalism in their preoccupation with categorisation for categorisation's sake. In one of the few studies to focus specifically on narrative *and* genre, Nick Lacey (2000) in fact treats the two as separate items, though he does include 'narrative and theme' in his account of genre.

For television scholars, the dominance of certain genres in the schedules has been seen as a barrier to innovation, but equally there has been some criticism of the diluting of genres, particularly where this is seen to marginalise or alienate their core audiences. Feminist scholars in particular have questioned the way in which British soaps have moved away from their traditional focus on relationships and dialogue to focus more on crime, violence and large-scale disasters, such as the notorious plane crash that removed most of the cast of the long-running soap *Emmerdale* in the late 1980s.

Recognising that the pleasures of formula and repetition offered by popular genres take us back to oral forms (Cobley 2014) where the reception of formula may be different each time it is performed, likewise suggests that it is lazy and superficial to simply dismiss genre narratives on the basis of vague and ill-defined notions of what constitutes art and innovation in storytelling. For television narratives in particular, which fulfill a 'bardic function' (Fiske and Hartley 1978) in contemporary society, we need to consider the specific context of the production and scheduling of shows, and how their structure both responds to and is shaped by viewing habits. John Ellis (1992) has argued that the tv schedule acts a kind of 'metanarrator' organising the televisual day so that schedulers, advertisers and audiences know where certain shows and genres will typically be found. The feminization of television (Ball 2012) discussed in the last chapter may have changed perceptions of which genres belong where. In addition, the proliferation of new channels since the advent of satellite and cable tv has meant that bespoke channels now cater for specific genres, for example, channels dedicated to cookery or lifestyle programmes or channels which only show reruns of situation comedies. Nevertheless, much prime-time television remains heavily formulaic, allowing for the particular format of the talent show or quiz to be endlessly reproduced and sold to other countries to produce their own versions. From a scheduler's or advertiser's point of view, these shows bring guaranteed audiences, while audiences know that each time they tune in they are guaranteed more of the kind of entertainment they enjoy. While cultural critics may bemoan the dominance of such formulaic fare, it is important to take into account both the industry perspective and that of the audience, for whom predictability and repetition may be necessary where watching tv takes place in the context of other activities and needs to be 'interruptible' (Modleski 1983).

Fan cultures also help to demonstrate not just the enduring appeal of popular genres, but the fact that the impulse to categorise is not confined to the entertainment industries or to genre scholars. Everywhere on fan sites we see classification and archiving of material by fans for fans, as well as the generation of new genres and subgenres, for example, slash fiction, cross-over fiction or real-person fic. By focusing more on the 'extratextual' aspects of genre, theorists can explore the pleasures of 'genre uncertainty' (Smith 2014) for audiences or examine how certain genres such as vampire or zombie narratives appear to dominate the cultural zeitgeist and help channel societal anxieties and preoccupations.

APPROACHES TO GENRE

HISTORY AND EVOLUTION

Most studies of genre begin by attempting to define the term and trace its historical antecedents, taking us back to classical antiquity and the evolution of terms for categorising literature (tragedy, epic, drama) that continue to be widely employed and taught into the present day. While it is argued that genres were seen as stable and universal in classical theory, with the Romantics the notion of genres as 'historically determined, dynamic entities' (Pyrhönen 2007: 111) emerges to offer an alternative to the 'tyrannical constraints upon an author's individual feeling and sensibility' (112) represented by traditional generic rules and norms. Formalism and structuralism are also important in the history of genre theory, with attempts to systematise the study of specific genres, as in Propp's *Morphology of the Folk Tale* (1928) or Todorov's studies of the fantastic (1975) and detective fiction (1977). Rather than being seen as barriers to innovation, genre here may be seen as necessary for us to understand what innovation means, while at the same time 'norms become visible thanks to such violations' (Pyrhönen 2007: 112).

Genre theory's attempts to avoid seeming rigid and inflexible have involved drawing on philosophical theories and terms, as in the appropriation of Wittgenstein's theory of 'family resemblances' in language, which has been used to explore genres not as discrete entities but as dynamic constructs shaped and responsive to what surrounds them (e.g. Fowler 1982). Other linguistic theories that have influenced contemporary genre studies include speech act theory (Austin 1962) and Bakhtin's (1986) concept of 'speech genres', both of which show that everyday conversation and language may also be understood in terms of recurring types and patterns, firmly rooting the idea of genre in the social and fixing attention on the impact that genre may have in both reflecting and helping to shape social formations.

While many accounts of genre trace a teleological path, showing the continuity and evolution of genres across time and an inevitable trajectory towards greater self-awareness, Jane Feuer (1992) argues, that for television at least, this is a misleading picture. Like many genre theorists, she is critical of the notion of genres as evolving naturally or inevitably, arguing instead that 'Genres are rhetorical and pragmatic constructions of an analyst, not acts of nature' (142). Focusing her analysis on the television sitcom, Feuer argues that contemporary shows display clear 'regression to earlier incarnations' (156), problematising the notion that genre is always about 'progressing toward a more perfect form' (156–7). She reminds us that television texts need to be understood not as discrete entities but as part of what Raymond Williams (1974) called the televisual 'flow', where programmes blend seamlessly into one another, aided by continuity announcements and the ease with which audiences are able to zap between channels.

DEFINING GENRES

Most studies of genre move from considering the issues and survey-ing the literature to providing in-depth discussion of a specific genre, identifying its characterising features and how that particular genre has evolved. For example in *Narrative and Genre*, Nick Lacey (2000) devises a matrix of setting, character, narrative, iconography, style and stars which he then applies to the crime and science fiction genres. Many studies define genre as much by what it is *not* as by what it is and recognise that genres are dynamic constructs that evolve over time. It is also important to acknowledge that not all genres are nar-rative: some would argue, for example, that much news discourse, as well as current affairs shows or music channels, have content that is clearly recognisable as belonging to a type without necessarily telling a story.

However, some theorists have focused their attention on trying to establish the various ways in which the concept of genre itself is defined. For example, film theorist Robert Stam (2000, cited by Chandler 1997) notes that:

> While some genres are based on story content (the war film), others are borrowed from literature (comedy, melodrama) or from other media (the musical). Some are performer-based (the Astaire-Rogers film) budget-based (blockbusters), while others are based on artistic status (the art film), racial identity (Black cinema), location (the Western) or sexual ori-entation (Queer cinema).
>
> (Stam 2000: 14)

Meanwhile David Bordwell (1989, also cited by Chandler 1997) focuses on genre as:

> Grouping by period or country (American films of the 1930s), by direc-tor or star or producer or writer or studio, by technical process (Cine-mascope films), by cycle (the 'fallen women' films), by series (the 007

movies), by style (German Expressionism), by structure (narrative), by ideology (Reaganite cinema), by venue ('drive-in movies'), by purpose (home movies), by audience ('teenpix'), by subject or theme (family film, paranoid-politics movies).

(Bordwell 1989: 148)

Narrative technique may provide a way of categorising texts by genre, for example, the 'first person shooter' in videogaming, the dialogue novel (Thomas 2012), nonlinear narratives or narratives featuring 'unnatural narration' (Richardson 2006). Where narrative technique is not the defining feature, nevertheless structure, mode of telling, point of view and so on are often crucial in establishing similarities and differences between texts grouped together by genre.

Genre theory has also engaged in its own attempts to categorise and define overarching aims and approaches. For example, Jane Feuer (1992) provides three labels for summarising existing approaches: the aesthetic, the ritual and the ideological. The aesthetic approach is focused on understanding genre in relation to individual artistic expression and the role of the author, the ritual approach 'sees genre as an exchange between industry and audience' (145) and the ideological approach 'views genre as an instrument of control' (145).

READERS AND AUDIENCES

Most contemporary accounts of genre focus not just on the text or how it is produced, but on reception and interpretation, and particularly the pleasures audiences derive from particular genres and the social functions and uses they have. This stems in part from an impatience with notions of genre which treat them 'as if they spring full-blown from the head of Zeus' (Altman 1984: 8) and the desire to acknowledge that reader competence is crucial to how genres are constructed and construed. Buckingham's (1993) work with child audiences showed how early these competences are developed, but theorists are also at pains to stress that audiences derive pleasure from seeing generic conventions being manipulated (Abercrombie 1996) and often engage in 'reading against the grain', for example, reading a science fiction narrative as a romance. Jason Mittell (2006) argues that for what he calls the 'boutique audience', only complex, challenging and 'rewatchable' television shows will do, with the pleasure being derived from deconstructing genre conventions and from engaging in metatextual discussion and analysis with other viewers via internet forums and social media.

GENRE ACROSS MEDIA

With the redefinition of genre as 'an abstract conception rather than something that exists empirically in the world' (Feuer 1992:144), the term can be useful for looking at narratives across media, where the conventions and norms may vary, but where audience expectations and engagement may extend to multiple media forms. A good example of this is the crime genre, which enjoys enduring popular appeal in film, television, videogames, fiction and graphic novels. Crime is also popular in new media narratives, as discussed in the next chapter, with one of the first examples of Twitterfiction (see Chapter 8) being Matt Richtel's experimentation with the 'twiller', a thriller unfolding over a series of tweets.

Crime fiction has enjoyed a loyal and devoted following from the early decades of the twentieth century, with subgenres evolving to cater to every taste, from the more cerebral clue-puzzle format, to serial killer narratives and revenge thrillers. As with other genres, some of the differences between the subgenres are stylistic. So hardboiled detective fiction tends to feature more graphic and gritty dialogue (Thomas 2012) in comparison to the more polite tones of the classic whodunit. But subgenres may also be defined by setting ('Nordic' or 'Tartan' Noir) or by the occupation of the protagonists (police procedural, private eye, forensic investigator). As with most popular genres, parodies and hybrids also emerge, allowing readers to take pleasure from the excesses and improbabilities of the form, as in Malcolm Pryce's series of 'Aberystwyth Noir' novels, including *Aberystwyth Mon Amour* (2001) and *Last Tango in Aberystwyth* (2003), which transpose the world of Raymond Chandler to a Welsh seaside town.

Scandinavian crime (also known as 'Nordic Noir') has enjoyed great popularity across fiction, film and television in recent years, with multiple adaptations of Stieg Larsson's Millennium trilogy and Henning Mankell's Wallander novels and television dramas *The Killing* (2007–12) and *The Bridge* (2011–) reinventing the genre with their focus on social realism (Thomas 2012) and their foregrounding of female protagonists. The television narratives in particular appear to break the mould of contemporary tv dramas by presenting viewers with slow-paced narratives characterised by acute attention to detail (Cobley 2014). Whereas many crime dramas offer viewers resolution and the revelation of 'whodunit' within an hour-long episode, the first season of *The Killing* ran for 20 hour-long episodes (with 2 episodes broadcast back-to-back in the UK), demanding a considerable commitment on the part of viewers but allowing for greater depth in characterisation and plotting.

In the UK, the sense of generic resemblance between these dramas was exacerbated by the fact that they were broadcast on the same channel (BBC4) at the same time (Saturday nights at 9), establishing this firmly in the minds of viewers as a time when quality, European crime drama would be on offer. Soon American remakes as well as other dramas shown on different networks emerged, emulating the style of these 'prestige' shows (Smith 2014), notably their use of wide shots to place the characters in distinctive settings and long takes where brooding silences could really be allowed to take hold.

GENRE UNCERTAINTY

In his discussion of *True Detective*, Smith (HBO, 2014 –) argues that the show's blending of detective and murder mystery elements offers the viewer a pleasing sense of disorientation, disrupting expectations and introducing fantastical, supernatural elements to destabilise the show's generic identity. Smith argues that *True Detective* shares this sense of uncertainty about what kind of show it is with other television narratives such as *Lost* (2004–10), *Twin Peaks* (1990–1) and *Top of the Lake* (2013–).

Smith's essay articulates the tension that the reader or viewer feels between wanting more of the experiences and sensations that a particular genre offers, but also wanting to be surprised and kept guessing. For Smith, the finale of *True Detective* disappointed because it removed the uncertainty that had been so much a part of his viewing pleasure. Endings often excite these strong reactions, as the likely outcome is often so heavily defined by genre. For example, we expect a romance to produce a happy ending, but contemporary varieties often set out to challenge and subvert these expectations, as in *500 Days of Summer* (2009), where at the end of the movie there is no prospect of a future for the relationship that is the main focus of the narrative.

ANALYSIS: REAL-LIFE NARRATIVES

Although discussion of real-life narratives in recent times has been dominated by the rise of 'reality tv', the popularity of the genre is also evident across cinema ('based on a true story'; cinema vérité) and 'true life' magazines (including titles such as *Closer, Reveal, That's Life*). The earliest novels attempted to create a strong sense of realism for readers, often purporting to tell a true story, and feigning to conceal revealing details about characters or locations as a ruse to make the reader feel that the story the secrets and intrigues they were made party to might actually have serious consequences for those involved. Modernist and postmodernist narratives set about to disrupt and fundamentally challenge notions of the real, reflecting greater cultural uncertainty about what could be assumed to be shared realities or truths. With Baudrillard's (1994) concept of the 'hyperreal' it is even suggested that modern readers and audiences have lost contact with any sense of the real, so dependent are they on mediated versions of experience. Many contemporary narratives, including reality tv, unashamedly revel in this idea of **hyperreality**, presenting audiences with 'constructed reality' shows and events where 'real people' deliver scripted dialogue and where media celebrities appear on our screens seemingly revealing intimate truths about themselves.

Nevertheless, new media platforms such as YouTube are testament to the enduring appeal of first person narrative accounts of life events, no matter how trivial, with the rawness of the emotions on display offering an intense affective experience for the viewer. Psychologists have been particularly interested in the life narrative as potentially offering a kind of healing, release, or therapy (e.g. Frank 1997), or 'recipes for structuring experience' which can result in shared understandings of the nature of a 'life' that become canonical (Bruner 2004). The question of whether such genres 'are built into the human genome' (Bruner 2004:697) has even been raised, with the focus being on identifying the forms these life stories may take as 'one important way of characterizing a culture is by the narrative models it makes available for describing the course of a life' (Bruner 2004: 694).

In her categorisation of different approaches to genre, Feuer (1992) defines the ritual approach as one in which the focus is on how 'a culture speaks to itself' (145). If we look at contemporary real-life narratives through this lens, then our narrative models would appear to privilege sensation and transformation, though it also has to be allowed that a focus on 'everydayness' is also evidence (Highmore 2001) in some varieties. For example, video diaries and Facebook updates may feature seemingly banal or trivial activities, while real-life magazines and reality television tend to focus more on crisis points in people's lives.

Structurally, as was discussed in Chapter 1, many real-life narratives follow the Proppian model of a hero overcoming obstacles with support from others before finally gaining recognition and attaining his or her sought-for prize. Talent shows, cookery competitions and the stories of overcoming adversity featured in real-life magazines all tend to follow this pattern. Reality tv is also interesting in terms of narrative time (discussed in Chapter 3), offering a close approximation of what Genette calls 'scene' where the time of narration is roughly equivalent to the time of the narrated events.

Adopting what Feuer (1992) calls an aesthetic approach to the genre, focusing on its conventions and mode of authorship, it is evident that real-life narratives, particularly on television, clearly draw on archetypes and patterns from folk and fairy tales, particularly the idea of the magical transformation of the hero. Lifestyle and make-over shows often have an expert or panel of experts to advise and guide the hero through this process, resulting in the big 'reveal' at the end of the show, where the dramatic transformation is shared with friends and family. Real-life narratives also share with folk tales a seemingly simple moral framework, setting heroes against villains and suggesting that the transformation of the hero makes him or her a better person, whether because he or she is more beautiful, slimmer or more skilled at DIY.

With reality tv, the increasing narrativisation of the format since the 1990s (Dovey 2008) has led to a more pronounced focus on 'characters' and their crises. As participants play up to the cameras, the notion of self as performance is constantly being reinscribed, with the real-life participants often going on to attain celebrity status as the boundaries between their on- and off-screen selves become more and more porous. The notion of the self as a project is particularly evident in makeover shows, where the idea of surveilling the self is perpetuated, as contestants and the experts who guide them are constantly watching and evaluating how they look and how they present themselves.

Described by one critic as a 'feral genre' (Hill 2007) that is constantly spawning new varieties, reality tv has come in for a lot of criticism, seen by some as nothing more than a modern day 'freak-show' (Dovey 2000) where the insecurities and desperate desire for attention of the participants is put on display for the audience's entertainment and gratification. Critics have also highlighted the ideological assumptions behind the privileging of 'liveness' on tv (Couldry 2004) and the fact that all they offer us is a 'folk theory' of the real (Ryan 2006).

What Feuer (1992) calls an ideological approach to the genre might therefore focus on the ways in which the audience are manipulated by the creators of these narratives into associating moral improvement with material possessions or accepting the notion that to be successful it may be necessary to overcome one's competitors whatever the costs. As Miller (2010) puts it, 'Reality TV is suffused with . . . avarice, possessive individualism, hyper-competitiveness, and commodification' (160). Problems and obstacles in this world-view are not social but individual, a matter of personal responsibility and thus easily overcome by perseverance, skill or sheer good luck. In the UK, reality tv has been particularly criticised for its depiction of class, with shows featuring working-class participants tending to portray them as undeserving and lazy, while shows featuring the upper classes portray their excesses as comical or even something to be aspired to.

An ideological approach also needs to understand the rise of reality tv in the context of wider changes affecting the television industry and society more broadly. As well as the obvious benefits from a commercial point of view of reproducing a tried-and-tested formula, cultural critics might point to the focus on 'ordinary' people as a rejection of authority figures or manufactured celebrities, while the appetite for real-time narratives might be understood in the context of the rise of new media which make it easier for us to keep up with events and communicate with each other seemingly instantaneously.

In his discussion of what he terms 'concurrent narration', where we 'tell as we live' rather than 'live now, tell later', Margolin (1999: 161) argues that this is part of a more general bias for 'life as lived' forms of narrative driven by the dominance of tv in contemporary culture. John Fiske's (1987) analysis of television's **'nowness'** has become especially influential in this regard, as it encapsulates the appeal of this focus on the moment and the way in which the audience is made to feel a part of the events they see depicted on their screens. Fiske argues that this isn't just about the fact that television is able to deliver 'live' events, but relates to how television narratives almost uniquely work their way into our everyday routines and lives and invites us to share in the emotions of those whose stories we follow over periods of months and even years.

However, as was said earlier, genre theory has increasingly embraced the idea that audiences are not just passive recipients of formulae that are endlessly being reproduced to keep them happy, but creative and critical participants in the process by which genres are continually being reinvented and made to reflect current social and cultural realities. Many reality tv shows invite audience participation through phone-ins and social media, while alongside the 'official' channels for communication audiences also create their own unofficial means of displaying their engagement or voicing their disquiet. As Ryan (2006) has argued, television audiences have a sophisticated understanding of camera effects, and how reality tv relies on scripting and intertextuality. Audiences of reality tv have also been said to display a default critical mode in relation to their own viewing habits (Hill 2008), criticising both the shows for their absurdities and contrived plot devices and themselves for putting up with these things.

Ryan's (2006) study of the US reality tv show *Survivor* is a welcome but rare intervention by a narrative theorist into studies of the genre. Nevertheless, narrative theory has a lot to contribute to discussions of the form, for example, providing terms and models for analysing the mode of narration or the structuring of events. There is scope for further work in this area, particularly with regards to the narratological concept of metalepsis (discussed in Chapter 3), where the boundaries between different narrative levels collapse, creating uncertainty or confusion over where the real and the fictional overlap.

CONCLUSION

The debate continues as to whether or not genre is a useful or relevant term for analysing twenty-first-century narratives. Certainly, as Abercrombie (1996) noted, at the very least 'the boundaries between genres are shifting and becoming more permeable' (46). Some might welcome this fluidity and dynamism, particularly in contexts such as television where the schedule can have a stultifying impact on what may or may not be shown at a particular time of day. However, the idea that genre conventions somehow inhibit innovation can easily be contested by pointing to the ways in which genres evolve, combine and recombine. In addition, as genre theory has engaged more and more with audiences, we can better understand why routine and familiarity may be an important aspect of the pleasure we derive from certain kinds of narrative. As we shall see in the next chapter, popular and long-established genres are prevalent in narratives emerging from new media forms, and so understanding how genre works, for writers, producers and audiences alike, continues to be an important area of study.

FOLLOW-UP ACTIVITIES

1. Try to identify common contemporary genres from the following sources:
   a) A television schedule online or in a print newspaper or magazine such as the *Radio Times*
   b) IMDB (www.imdb.com)
   c) Amazon (books, videogames, DVDs/Blu-ray)
2. Write your life story in a paragraph (adapted from Green and LeBihan 1996). *After* you have written your paragraph, consider the following:
   a) Did you begin 'I was born . . .'?
   b) Did you include material on school, family, location?
   c) How did you end your story?
   d) Why did you spend more time on some parts of your story than others?

SUGGESTED READING

Nick Lacey's *Narrative and Genre* examines genre theory alongside narratological models and is illustrated with contemporary examples from tv and film. Jane Feuer's chapter 'Genre Study and Television' examines different approaches to genre, with specific reference to the television situation comedy. *The Television Genre Book* provides a comprehensive range of essays on a wide variety of tv genres and includes a good introductory chapter on genre theory. Heta Pyrhö-nen's chapter on genre from *The Cambridge Companion to Narrative* offers a more explicitly narratological focus and an analysis of the classic detective genre. Jason Mittell has written extensively about contemporary television genres, drawing on narratological terms and models.

REFERENCES

Abercrombie, N. (1996) *Television and Society*. Cambridge: Polity Press.

Altman, R. (1984) A Semantic/Syntactic Approach to Film Genre. *Cinema Journal*, 23(3), 6–18.

Austin, J.L. (1962) *How to Do Things with Words*. Oxford: Oxford University Press.

Bakhtin, M.M. (1986) *Speech Genres and Other Late Essays*. Transl. V.W. McGee. Austin: University of Texas Press.

Ball, V. (2012) The 'Feminization' of British Television and the Re-Traditionali-zation of Gender. *Feminist Media Studies*, 12(2), 248–64.

Baudrillard, J. (1994) *Simulacra and Simulacrum*. Transl. S.F. Glaser. Ann Arbor: University of Michigan Press.

Bordwell, D. (1989) *Making Meaning: Inference and Rhetoric in the Interpretation of Cinema*. Cambridge, MA: Harvard University Press.

Bruner, J. (2004) Life as Narrative. *Social Research*, 71(3), 691–710.

Buckingham, D. (1993) *Children Talking Television: The Making of Television Literacy*. London: Falmer Press.

Chandler, D. (1997) An Introduction to Genre Theory. Accessed 20/3/15 at http://www.aber.ac.uk/media/Documents/intgenre/chandler_genre_theory.pdf

Cobley, P. (2014) (2nd ed.) *Narrative*. London: Routledge.

Couldry, N. (2004) Liveness, 'Reality', and the Mediated Habitus from Television to the Mobile Phone. *Communication Review*, 7(4), 353–61.

Creeber, G. (2008) (2nd ed.) *The Television Genre Book*. Basingstoke: Palgrave.

Derrida, J. (1990[1980]) The Law of Genre. In *Acts of Literature*, ed. D. Attridge, transl. A. Ronell. New York: Routledge.

Dovey, J. (2000) *Freakshow: First Person Media and Factual Television*. London: Pluto Press.

Dovey, J. (2008) Introduction. Reality TV. In *The Television Genre Book*, ed. G. Creeber. Basingstoke: Palgrave, 134–6.

Ellis, J. (1992) *Visible Fictions*. London: Routledge.

Feuer, J. (1992) Genre Study and Television. In *Channels of Discourse: Reassembled* (2nd ed.), ed. R.C. Allen. London: Routledge.

Fiske, J. (1987) *Television Culture*. London: Routledge.

Fiske, J. and Hartley, J. (1978) *Reading Television*. London: Methuen.

Fowler, A. (1982) *Kinds of Literature: An Introduction to the Theory of Genres and Modes*. Cambridge, MA: Harvard University Press.

Frank, A. (1997) *The Wounded Storyteller: Body, Illness and Ethics*. Chicago: University of Chicago Press.

Green, K. and LeBihan, J. (1996) *Critical Theory and Practice*. London: Routledge.

Highmore, B. (2001) (ed.) *The Everyday Life Reader*. London: Routledge.

Hill, A. (2007) *Restyling Factual TV: Audiences and News, Documentary and Reality Genres*. London: Routledge.

Hill, A. (2008) Audiences and Reality TV. In *The Television Genre Book* (2nd ed.), ed. G. Creeber. Basingstoke: Palgrave, 137.

Lacey, N. (2000) *Narrative and Genre*. Basingstoke: Macmillan.

Margolin, U. (1999) Of What Is Past, Is Passing, or to Come: Temporality, Aspectuality, Modality and the Nature of Literary Narrative. In *Narratologies: New Perspectives on Narrative Analysis*, ed. D. Herman. Columbus: Ohio State University Press, 142–66.

Miller, T. (2010) *Television Studies: The Basics*. London: Routledge.

Mittell, J. (2006) Narrative Complexity in Contemporary American Television. *The Velvet Light Trap*, 58, 29–40.

Modleski, T. (1983) The Rhythms of Reception: Daytime Television and Women's Work. In *Regarding Television: Critical Approaches – an Anthology*, ed. E.A. Kaplan. Frederick, MD: University Publications of America.

Neale, S. (2008) Studying Genre. In *The Television Genre Book*, ed. G. Creeber. Basingstoke: Palgrave, 3–5.

Propp, V. (2003[1928]) *Morphology of the Folk Tale*. Transl. L. Scott. Austin: University of Texas Press.

Pyrhönen, H. (2007) Genre. In *The Cambridge Companion to Narrative*, ed. D. Herman. Cambridge: Cambridge University Press, 109–23.

Richardson, B. (2006) *Unnatural Voices: Extreme Narration in Modern and Contemporary Fiction*. Columbus: Ohio State University Press.

Ryan, M-L. (2006) *Avatars of Story*. Minneapolis: University of Minnesota Press.

Smith, A.N. (2014) *True Detective* and the Pleasures of Genre Uncertainty. *CST Online*. Accessed 20/3/15 at http://cstonline.tv/true-detective-and-the-pleasures-of-genre-uncertainty

Stam, R. (2000) *Film Theory*. Oxford: Blackwell.

Thomas, B. (2012) *Fictional Dialogue: Speech and Conversation in the Modern and Postmodern Novel*. Lincoln: University of Nebraska Press.

Todorov, T. (1975) *The Fantastic: A Structural Approach to a Literary Genre*. Ithaca: Cornell University Press.

Todorov, T. (1977) The Typology of Detective Fiction. In *The Poetics of Prose*. Transl. R. Howard. Oxford: Blackwell, 42–52.

Williams, R. (1974) *Television: Technology and Cultural Form*. London: Fontana.

8

NEW MEDIA NARRATIVES

'We are who we are and we see ourselves in brief light but live always in the shadow of what comes next.'

(Joyce 2001: 81)

Digital technologies have revolutionised the way we tell and consume stories. Admittedly, in some parts of the world access to these technologies cannot be taken for granted, and so traditional modes of oral storytelling may still hold sway. But if you walk around towns and cities in most affluent industrialised nations, you will see people consuming content, often in the form of stories, via smartphones, tablets and soon, perhaps, virtual reality headsets. Some commentators would go so far as to say that one of the major changes and innovations that digital technologies have brought is the ability for people to personalise and customise this content, even to generate their own content, telling their stories via Instagram, YouTube or Twitter. It also appears that new technologies offer us more opportunities to access stories on the move and to follow and share stories across multiple platforms.

One of the fundamental questions this raises is whether we need new narrative models to account for the changes in the way people tell, consume and recirculate stories in the digital age. Certainly, as Ciccoricco (2014) puts it, 'there is . . . much to be gained from what digital fiction can tell us about narrative and literary theory' (39). Is it the 'same' story if it is experienced via a handheld device as opposed to a hardback book or a flat screen tv? Can we still hold on to the distinction between author and reader in the age of the 'prosumer', where it is so easy to publish content and share our stories with the wider world? And is the whole concept of a text outdated where we may be talking about a Wikipedia entry that is constantly being edited or a tweet which disappears into a constantly updated timeline?

ELECTRONIC 'HYPERTEXT' FICTION

Even more radical are the challenges posed by so-called 'born digital' narratives that respond to and make use of the affordances of new technologies. In the 1980s, writers began to experiment with the possibilities opened up by hypertextual links in digital media. Pioneers of **hypertext fiction** such as Michael Joyce and Stuart Moulthrop played with the notion of allowing the reader to choose how he or she would 'navigate' the fiction, making each reading unique and unrepeatable, and radically unsettling the notion that stories have a fixed and identifiable plot.

It was to narratologists such as Roland Barthes that early theorists of electronic fiction looked, resurrecting debates about the 'death of the Author' and reviving terms such as the 'lexia', first used by Barthes in his attempt to free the text and offer the reader a more active role in constructing its meanings (as discussed in Chapters 2 and 5). Electronic texts fundamentally challenged our book-based notions of narrative as they weren't structured in terms of chapters, paragraphs and pages, but lexias and branching pathways that no trail of breadcrumbs could guarantee we could retrace.

Electronic texts depended on the technology of the day, and so writers, readers, educators and librarians had to respond quickly to the 'planned obsolescence' (Fitzpatrick 2011) of the technologies on which they relied. The online publisher of 'serious hypertext', Eastgate, devised its own 'writing environment', Storyspace, available for both Mac and Windows – but at a cost. In the early days of hypertext fiction, readers relied on floppy disks, then CD-ROMs, and it could be frustrating trying to find compatible versions, as in some cases they were only made available for one operating system.

Later hypertexts, such as Caitlin Fisher's *These Waves of Girls* (2001), were freely available via the web, bypassing the whole idea of the traditional gatekeepers, such as publishers, editors, marketers and so on. Fisher's hypertext was also more multimodal than the early works, incorporating sound, image and video, making it even more difficult to talk about the experience in any simplistic sense as 'reading'.

Marie-Laure Ryan, one of the most preeminent of new media narratologists, has written extensively about interactive fiction and the possibilities it opens up (e.g. Ryan 2001, 2006). However, she has also been vocal in challenging the 'hype about hypertext' (Ryan 2002), arguing that it is rarely read by anyone other than university professors. Recent reappraisals by 'third-wave' critics such as Astrid Ensslin (2007) and Alice Bell (2010) propose that a different approach is required, not, as in the case of first- and second-wave critics, comparing electronic fiction to its print predecessors or talking about it only in the abstract, but providing close analysis of the writing in the context of the affordances of the specific technologies on which it depends. Third-wave criticism is also characterised by the fact that it might just as easily draw parallels with videogames or multiplayer role-playing games as with traditional print-based prose fiction. Nevertheless, third-wave critics also remain deeply indebted to classical narratology, drawing on the work of Genette as well as Barthes in accounting for some of the particular features of interactive fiction such as the use of the second person 'you' (Bell and Ensslin 2011).

There is also evidence to suggest that many of the techniques pioneered by hypertext writers are now influencing digital narratives such as webdocs, where branching structures and interactive features allow users to dig deeper into news stories and the people caught up in them. For example, The Shirt on Your Back (http://interactive.guim.co.uk/next-gen/world/ng-interactive/2014/apr/bangladesh-shirt-on-your-back/) is an interactive documentary inviting the user to explore how garments sold in the UK are produced, focusing on the individual stories of people working in the factories while linking the time spent navigating the site to the wages they earn and the profits made by the retailers. Using the second person here implicates the user in the exploitation of the workers, while the interactive features powerfully drive home the injustice of the gap between the workers' earnings and the retailers' profits.

LUDOLOGY vs. NARRATOLOGY

The gamelike quality of many of these interactive forms of narrative has led to intense and at times heated debate about the extent to which videogames can be discussed alongside cinematic or literary forms of narrative. Espen Aarseth (1997) has coined the term 'ergodic literature' for forms where the intervention of the player/user is crucial and where the experience of the player is of events unfolding in real time with a variety of possible outcomes. According to this view, videogames contain storylike elements or narrative pretexts that provide the context for the game play, but this may be largely confined to certain segments such as the nonplayable 'cut scenes' which are much closer to narrative forms such as film. However, as we shall see, videogames are by no means the only form of narrative where questions of structure and control/freedom arise.

It has often been argued that contemporary games are moving more and more in the direction of adopting narrative, even novelistic techniques: for example, in the survival game *The Last of Us* (2013) the reader is made privy to the central characters' internal thoughts by means of voice-over. In addition, many videogames build on existing storyworlds and genre conventions familiar from television and cinema, for example, *L.A. Noire* (2011), or *Max Payne* (2008), which both draw on the urban thriller. Some contemporary games have even been argued to play with metafictional devices to encourage audiences 'to engage creatively with narrative meaning' (Ensslin 2012: 143), creating a new category of 'fictional literary art games' (144) or 'ludic-literary hybrids' (Ensslin 2014: 77). The terms 'ludo-narrativism' and 'ludo-narratology' have also been coined (Ensslin 2014: 83) to try to combine approaches from game design and game play with the more traditional focus on language and textuality from classical narratology.

LOCATION-BASED AND MOBILE STORYTELLING

Reading or viewing narratives on the go has become a lot easier with devices such as the Kindle, the iPad and the smartphone. In Japan, forms such as the keitai shousetsu, or cell phone novel, have emerged, while mobisodes condense episodes from popular tv shows in formats that can be enjoyed while on the move. Smartphones with geolocation apps also make it possible for users to share where they are with friends and family, uploading pictures or videos or tracking their journeys via maps or check-in apps such as Foursquare. Many apps now exist allowing users to access stories and information as they travel around sites of historical or literary interest, for example Shakespeare's London, potentially enhancing the special 'sense of place' that writers have attempted to create for centuries.

PARTICIPATORY NARRATIVES

Whereas 'born digital' narratives rely on a certain amount of technological know-how from both creators and audiences, the idea of **participatory narratives** celebrates the potential of contemporary online cultures to allow users to generate and share content freely. In his groundbreaking study, Henry Jenkins (2006b) defines a participatory culture as one which has 'relatively low barriers to artistic expression and civic engagement'. The idea of community is also important for Jenkins, providing 'strong support for creating and sharing one's creations with others' and where members of that community 'feel some degree of social connection with one another'. Participation may take many forms: according to Jenkins, 'Not every member must contribute, but all must believe they are free to contribute when ready and that what they contribute will be appropriately valued'. More and more, narrative texts may be experienced in ways which facilitate audience participation, for example, sing-along screenings of movies such as *Mamma Mia* (2008) or Secret Cinema events, offering an 'immersive experience' with life size recreations of movie sets for participants to explore.

Jenkins's work mainly relates to fan cultures, and in his book *Textual Poachers* (1992) he attempted to debunk prevailing stereotypes of fans as geekish obsessives, claiming instead that their creative engagement with the objects of their devotion should be applauded. Fan cultures have developed their own language and unique forms of narrative. For example, cross-over fiction might 'cross' characters from a classic novel, say Darcy and Elizabeth from Jane Austen's *Pride and Prejudice*, with characters from a contemporary media franchise such as *Buffy the Vampire Slayer*. Alternate universe fiction takes familiar characters and places them in a new and unexpected setting, for example stories where Darcy and Elizabeth are attending a US high school or the characters from the Harry Potter series are transported to an alien planet.

Content produced by fans is collaboratively curated and archived on fan sites, for example organising stories by genre, character pairings, or a rating system based on the extent to which 'adult' content is featured. While fan cultures are often celebrated as 'democratic' (Pugh 2005), 'fan-tagonisms' (Johnson 2007) can emerge, and fansites, like other websites, can be subject to bullying and factional disputes. While fanfiction has been dismissed as derivative, mainstream media outlets certainly seem to be drawing on many of the staples of the form, producing more and more spin-offs, prequels and the like, and offering users and consumers more and more opportunities to personalise and interact with content.

In the new media narrative marketplace, originality and the purity of the fictional world are perhaps less important than the ability of fans to customise, share and create their own content. This has led to the emergence of concepts such as that of the 'metaverse' (Sconce 2004) for popular franchises such as *Star Trek* or *Star Wars*, where the emphasis is on a continually expanding fictional world collaboratively produced by fans and their extratextual practices. Fan cultures have also been celebrated as being 'inherently, if metaphorically, metaleptic' (Turk 2011: 100), transgressing all sorts of boundaries, including that between the real and the fictional. Thus while terms and models from narrative theory can be useful in helping us to identify and understand some of these complex practices, in turn those practices also require that we refine and expand those terms and question many of our fundamental assumptions about the nature of narrative.

NARRATIVES FOR A CONVERGENCE CULTURE

Henry Jenkins also introduced the term 'convergence culture' (2006a) to describe a contemporary media landscape 'where "old" and "new" technologies collide', where content flows across different platforms and is generated by both grassroots and 'official' producers. The concept has been particularly influential in discussing news media, as users rely less and less on a single source of information, for example, a daily newspaper or a public broadcaster, and instead access the news across a range of sources and platforms, on their smartphones, via social media, blogs etc. The phenomenon of citizen journalism refers to the idea that ordinary citizens are now telling the stories of wars, uprisings and catastrophes, bypassing the traditional gatekeepers and governmental censors to provide others with raw but powerful insights into unfolding world events.

While increased convergence may have contributed to the rise of vast media franchises that span multiple platforms, at the same time it opens up the possibility of users accessing content outside of the mainstream and in ways that cannot always be controlled. In the past, television viewers were at the mercy of the schedulers, or metanarrators (Ellis 1992), shaping how programmes were grouped together and targeted at specific audiences. With the advent of video and DVD recording and on-demand services, viewers can access their favourite tv shows when and where they choose. The phenomenon of 'binge watching', for example, allows viewers to watch an entire series in one sitting. This has repercussions for the idea of gap filling discussed earlier (Chapter 5), whereby viewers use their imaginations to anticipate what might happen next and engage in discussion about possible plot outcomes and cliffhangers.

New technologies have also arguable affected attitudes towards the idea of plot, with spoiler websites now offering audiences the chance to read about future developments, as well as allowing them to 'spoil' things for others (see more on this later in the chapter). Jenkins (2007) has referred to contemporary media consumers as modern day hunters and gatherers, ranging across the internet collecting information and new content that they can then share with others.

DISTRIBUTED NARRATIVES AND SOCIAL MEDIA

For Jill Walker (2004), new media technologies facilitate a new kind of **distributed narrative**, where stories are fragmented, spread across media and accessed at different times and from different places by users. According to Walker, distributed narratives 'ask to be taken up, passed on and distributed' by users, radically challenging the idea of narrative as something that can be bounded or contained.

The phenomenon of Twitterfiction provides an interesting example of the contemporary distributed or 'networked' narrative (Page et al. 2013). Twitter is a social media platform which restricts users to content of 140 characters or less. Although initially Twitter was seen as a form of social media best suited for the distribution of news, by

February 2015 the site featured the tag line 'Start Telling Your Story' as its mission statement. The strong suggestion here is that everyone has a story to tell, and that Twitter is a good way to experiment with sharing stories with others in our network of friends and contacts.

From the outset, users found creative ways to overcome the seeming limitations of the 140-character limit and to imaginatively engage with the affordances of the form. Spoof and parody accounts for celebrity and historical figures abound, and Twitter accounts have also been created for characters and storyworlds connected with transmedia storytelling franchises. For example, users can follow the musings of the television character Don Draper from *Mad Men* via Twitter, and fans of the *Hunger Games* can sign up as citizens of Panem for an account set up in the name of The Capitol.

Other, more established writers have also used Twitter as a platform to distribute and share their writing, including novelists such as Jennifer Egan and David Mitchell. Tim Burton and Neil Gaiman have experimented with collaborative stories told via Twitter, and many accounts have been set up to retell well-known tales, including stories from the Bible and literary classics such as James Joyce's *Ulysses*.

For many writers, the challenge of composing a memorable and engaging story in 140 characters is a test of their creative powers. Canadian author Arjun Basu has coined the term the 'twister' to refer to the particular genre of short fiction he creates, tweeting daily twisters to his many followers, rehearsing a familiar theme involving two characters (assumed to be a man and a woman) experiencing some kind of dilemma or disruption in their relationship, as in the following example:

@arjunbasu – Feb 4
The movie ended and we hesitated to ruin what had been a successful first date and then I touched her hair, and coated it in popcorn butter.

Followers of Basu can expect to receive on average at least one story per day, and so a welcome sense of routine and familiarity is built up for his followers over time.

Even though Nelles (2012) reminds us that 'there have always been artists willing to risk the miniature' (87), Twitter nevertheless presents its own unique challenges and demands for the storyteller, as stories such as Basu's have to compete with all the other information appearing in the user's timeline and will continually be shared and spread across the Twittersphere by retweeters.

More complex still are forms of Twitterfiction relying on serialisation and an ongoing unfolding of the narrative over time. As discussed in Chapter 6, serial forms of narrative focus more on process rather than outcomes, creating a strong sense of engagement with the characters and the events they participate in as they are recounted over long periods of time.

In his retelling of the Indian epic the Mahabarata on @epicretold, Chindu Sreedharan draws on familiar techniques such as the cliffhanger to encourage his readers to read on and come back for more. In the following extract telling of one such dramatic incident, the tweets are represented as they would appear in the Twitter timeline (i.e. in reverse chronological order).

@epicretold 1 May
Seeing the water was too deep for the chariot to cross safely, I got down.
It was better that I went alone from here anyway.

@epicretold 30 Apr
He was eyeing the tributary of Ganga that blocked our path. Uncle Vidura's men had helped us across in a boat the night of our escape.

@epicretold 30 Apr
'Should we try to cross here?' Visoka's doubtful voice cut into my thoughts.

However, drawing on his experience as a journalist, Sreedharan also makes use of the affordances of Twitter, maintaining an ongoing dialogue with his followers and asking for their feedback on how the story is going, and foregrounding action and the 'newsworthiness' of his story to keep his followers wanting more.

Twitterfiction such as @epicretold relies on creating the experience of 'nowness' discussed in Chapter 7, placing us in the position of witnessing unfolding events, told in the present tense, embedded in the flow of our individual timelines which are constantly being updated. Such narratives rely on creating a sense of urgency and being in the moment for followers, responding to and exploiting the affordances of social media to maximum effect.

Walker also sees distributed narratives as having the potential to cross over into our daily lives, something which Twitterfiction clearly does, competing as it does with news updates, celebrity gossip etc. Increasingly, new media narratives play with the boundaries between fiction and reality, for example, by generating emails or SMS alerts that seem to come from the characters within a fictional world or by using Facebook profiles to gather real-world information about us which can then be embedded in the work of fiction.

Stories told on social media challenge many of our fundamental assumptions about narrative, particularly the notions of linearity and sequence, while also moving away from the model of the single teller towards the idea of coproduction and new forms of cotellership (Page et al. 2013). Sharing and linking multimodal content also represents a challenge for narrative theory in terms of defining what counts as a core part of the story as opposed to material which is incidental or peripheral. Even concepts such as context become complex where the context of the telling and the context of the reception of the story may be fluid, moving between online and offline environments. Whereas traditional models of narrative tend to refer to narrator and reader as fairly stable entities who control the direction of the story, in networked environments both the distribution and reception of material is virtually impossible to manage as so much depends on the contingencies of when and how that material is accessed and shared.

TRANSMEDIA STORYTELLING

With increasing convergence between media and the emergence of new platforms allowing users to generate and link story content, the idea of narrative as something that is attributable to a single source becomes increasingly problematic. A whole raft of terms exists for attempting to map this new landscape, each being constantly contested and redefined. In the field of narratology, the terms transmediality (Ryan 2013) and intermediality (Grishakova and Ryan 2010)

are preferred; these terms concern themselves with medium speci-
ficity and definitions of medium as much as tracing how stories may
migrate or flow across media. In media theory, the term **transmedia
storytelling** has become more widely used, though not without
controversy and ongoing debate about its definition and usage.

Henry Jenkins (2011) defines transmedia storytelling as 'a process where integral elements of a fiction get dispersed systematically
across multiple delivery channels for the purpose of creating a unified and coordinated entertainment experience'. In attempting to
distinguish the concept from that of branding or franchising, Jenkins
adds that 'each medium makes its own unique contribution to the
unfolding of the story', for example, by providing more backstory for
minor characters, offering us new perspectives on events and deep-
ening audience engagement. Jenkins stresses that in his understanding transmedia storytelling is about 'expanded potential', potential
which includes the input of audiences and fans as much as what may
have been designed or imagined by authors and producers. Jenkins
is also at pains to identify historical antecedents, including the works
of Tolkien, L. Frank Baum and Disney, and to include figures and
storylines from the press and current affairs, arguing that 'Obama is
as much a transmedia character as Obi Wan is'.

While Jenkins is opposed to the notion of any kind of formula
for transmedia storytelling, he highlights the importance of what
he calls 'radical intertextuality' and multimodality for his use of the
term, as well as the idea that content flows across media. In his discussions, Jenkins has used *The Matrix*, *Lost* and *Heroes* as examples
of transmedia storytelling, but he is also keen to include 'grassroots'
examples of the kind generated by 'decisions made in teenagers'
bedrooms' (2013). Nevertheless, critics are sceptical about the ways
in which the term has been applied. For example, Mike Jones (2011)
takes issue with the 'Empty, vacuous, ignorant, presumptive, absurd
and facile weasel-word statements' that surround the term, arguing
that by stressing how radical and revolutionary transmedia storytelling is we neglect the ways in which it connects with the traditions
and foundations of storytelling. Jones (2012) also rails against the
lazy appropriation of the term to refer to any kind of media campaign that happens to be distributed across different platforms without giving any thought to 'key narrative and audience experience
questions'.

PARATEXTS AND NARRATIVE EXTENSIONS

In his analysis of the contemporary media landscape, Jonathan Gray (2010) draws on Genette's (1997) concept of the **paratext**. In Genette's use of the term, the focus is on the variety of materials that surround a literary text which act as a 'threshold' to that text, for example, prefaces, dedications, table of contents pages and so on. Setting out to examine 'how meaning and value are constructed outside of what we have often considered to be the text itself' (ix), Gray extends Genette's term to argue that paratexts do more than start texts, they 'also create and continue them' (11). Thus he shows how trailers, posters and cast interviews help generate and stimulate expectations of films and tv shows before they are aired, while websites, role-playing games or studio tours might allow audiences to extend their engagement with the characters and storylines associated with a particular storyworld long after they have finished with the book, film or videogame where they were first encountered. Gray demonstrates how media paratexts, far from being peripheral, are 'a central part of media production and consumption processes' (16), so that if we ignore them, our understanding of the cultures of production and consumption will be impoverished. In Gray's usage paratexts are 'the greeters, gatekeepers and cheerleaders for and of the media' (17), leading to an increased focus on the multiplicity of ways in which audiences may engage with a narrative in the digital era.

Paratextual approaches have been criticised for being little more than exercises in analysing the marketing of cultural products. In addition, Doherty (2014) has accused the 'paratextual cohort' of devoting so much time and energy to the 'distracting digital clutter' that they ignore 'the prize in the box', namely the core text for which the paratext is the 'decorative wraparound material'. Nevertheless, more and more critical attention is being paid to paratextual material across a wide range of disciplines and is closely related to the increased focus on worldbuilding (Wolf 2012) and transmediality in the contemporary media marketplace.

Together with Jason Mittell, Gray (2007) has written about the phenomenon of the 'spoiler', whereby fans reveal plot details online. They discuss the spoiler in the context of the changing nature of transmedia storytelling, arguing that contemporary audiences may be less concerned with plot outcomes than with how the narrative is constructed and that 'How viewers wish to experience narratology unfolding can vary'. As part of their research, Gray and Mittell conducted a survey to draw on the experiences of users of discussions forums and to better understand how spoiler communities might operate. This focus on readers, audiences and users of contemporary narratives is becoming increasingly prevalent in postclassical, particularly as new media narratives make these kinds of responses more visible and accessible.

NARRATIVE MASHUPS

The phenomenon of the mashup brings together content from different sources to produce a new output. YouTube is full of mashups based on remixing or sampling tracks and videos from multiple musical artists or bands. The effect can be to identify new resonances and melodic echoes, but equally the results may be deliberately dissonant and provocative. YouTube also has lots of examples of movie and tv mashups, for example, a trailer which brings together two media franchises – the *Saw* horror movies and *Wallace and Gromit*, an animation series mainly aimed at children (https://www.youtube.com/watch?v=kvWAxH3EQus). Literary forms of the mashup also exist, for example, *Pride and Prejudice and Zombies* (2009) by Seth Grahame-Smith, which combines the original text of Jane Austen's novel with all the blood and gore of a zombie narrative.

Booth (2012) has argued that mashups are 'a pattern of contemporary media development' (10–11), not just a thing, but a process, a way of looking at today's media environment. In particular, he writes about the ways in which contemporary television narratives 'mashup' characteristics of online media, from the use of Twitter hashtags to invite participation and debate, to Tumblr-like pastiches and parodies of other media on shows such as *Community* (NBC 2009). The mashup may also produce temporal displacement, combining footage from past and present, or the past and the future, making it impossible purely to focus on the one text or cultural product in terms of its meaning or cultural value and posing some challenges to notions such as quality or taste, as the classical and the contemporary, high and low cultures are relentlessly 'mashed' together.

CONCLUSION

When I coedited a volume of essays called 'New Narratives' in 2011, one of the contributors quipped that by the time it was published it should have been renamed 'Old Narratives' as so much had changed in the intervening period. I have also learned that it is dangerous to label anything as 'new', as literary and cultural historians will nearly always point to precursors and antecedents. Nevertheless, over the last 15 years my consumption and understanding of narrative has been radically reshaped by the innovations made possible by digital technologies. The word 'revolution' may be overused in this context, but many of the new media narratives discussed in this chapter do raise fundamental questions about the nature of narrative and the relevance of basic concepts such as those of authorship, plot or text in the context of the constant remixing, remediation and rebooting of stories that is so typical of our daily experience of narrative in the present day. Yet narrative theory and the terms and models derived from classical narratology remain crucial for our navigation of these new forms and experiences, with long-neglected terms such as Genette's concept of the paratext finding new purpose and meaning in ways which he could surely never have envisaged. These are exciting times for the study of narrative and for anyone interested not just in charting these new forms as they emerge, but in exploring narrative as a methodology for understanding the wider cultural practices of which they form a part.

FOLLOW-UP ACTIVITIES

1. Analyse the paratexts for a contemporary narrative (e.g. film, videogame, tv show, novel). For example, you might choose a movie trailer, a Twitter account for a tv character or an interview with an author. What do these paratexts add to your enjoyment and understanding of the primary text?

2. Choose a narrative that you have enjoyed recently and explore how the text has been reimagined as fanfiction or a fanvid.

3. Explore how audiences have reacted to a recent movie release or tv show on social media. For example, you might do a hashtag search or look for Tumblr pages set up by fans.

SUGGESTED READING

The website for the New Media Writing Prize (www.newmediaw ritingprize.co.uk) has lots of examples of interactive fiction, and the Electronic Literature Consortium maintains and updates its own directory (http://directory.eliterature.org). Online blogs by Henry Jenkins (www.henryjenkins.org), Jason Mittell (https://justtv.word press.com) and Jonathan Gray (http://www.extratextual.tv/tag/ paratexts/) are an invaluable resource for scholarship in this field.

New Narratives: Stories and Storytelling in the Digital Age has contributions by some of the leading practitioners and theorists of new media narratives, including Michael Joyce, Marie-Laure Ryan and Nick Montfort. Alice Bell and Astrid Ensslin also have chapters in this volume on hypertext fiction, and are the editors of *Analyzing Digital Fiction*, a more recent volume which includes my own chapter on Twitterfiction. Marie-Laure Ryan is one of the key theorists of media and digital narratives, and has recently coedited a volume of essays with Jan Noël Thon called *Storyworlds across Media*.

As well as work in media and cultural studies, fan studies also provides an important resource for understanding emerging trends and practices in online environments. As well as the work of Henry Jenkins, the Organization for Transformative Works (www.transforma tiveworks.org) provides some useful resources and publishes its own journal.

REFERENCES

Aarseth, E. (1997) *Cybertext: Perspectives on Ergodic Literature*. Baltimore: Johns Hopkins University Press.

Bell, A. (2010) *The Possible Worlds of Hypertext Fiction*. Basingstoke: Palgrave.

Bell, A. and Ensslin, A. (2011) 'I know what it was. You know what it was:' Second Person Narration in Hypertext Fiction. *Narrative*, 19(3), 311–29.

Bell, A. and Ensslin, A. (2014) *Analyzing Digital Fiction*. London: Routledge.

Booth, P. (2012) *Time on TV: Temporal Displacement and Mashup Television*. New York: Peter Lang.

Ciccoricco, D. (2014) Digital Fiction and Worlds of Perspective. In *Analyzing Digital Fiction*, eds. A. Bell, A. Ensslin and H. Rustad. London: Routledge, 39–56.

Doherty, T. (2014) The Paratext's Thing. *The Chronicle of Higher Education*. Accessed 23/3/15 at http://chronicle.com/article/The-Paratexts-the-Thing/143761/

Ellis, J. (1992) *Visible Fictions*. London: Routledge.

Ensslin, A. (2007) *Canonizing Hypertext*. London: Continuum.

Ensslin, A. (2012) *The Language of Gaming*. Basingstoke: Palgrave.

Ensslin, A. (2014) Playing with Rather than by the Rules: Metaludicity, Allusive Fallacy, and Illusory Agency in *The Path*. In *Analyzing Digital Fiction*, eds. A. Bell, A. Ensslin and H. Rustad. London: Routledge, 75–93.

Fitzpatrick, K. (2011) *Planned Obsolescence: Publishing, Technology and the Future of the Academy*. New York: New York University Press.

Genette, G. (1997[1987]) *Paratexts*. Transl. J. Lewin. Cambridge: Cambridge University Press.

Gray, J. (2010) *Show Sold Separately: Promos, Spoilers and Other Media Paratexts*. New York: New York University Press.

Gray, J. and Mittell, J. (2007) Speculation on Spoilers: *Lost* Fandom, Narrative Consumption and Rethinking Textuality. *Participations* 4(1). Accessed 20/3/15 at http://www.participations.org/Volume%204/Issue%201/4_01_graymittell.htm

Grishakova, M. and Ryan, M-L. (eds.) (2010) *Intermediality and Storytelling*. Berlin: DeGruyter.

Jenkins, H. (1992) *Textual Poachers: Television Fans and Participatory Culture*. London: Routledge.

Jenkins, H. (2006a) *Convergence Culture: Where Old and New Media Collide*. New York University Press.

Jenkins, H. (2006b) Confronting the Challenges of Participatory Culture: Media Education for the 21st Century (Part One). Accessed 20/3/15 at http://henryjenkins.org/2006/10/confronting_the_challenges_of.html

Jenkins, H. (2007) Transmedia Storytelling 101. Accessed 20/3/15 at http://henryjenkins.org/2007/03/transmedia_storytelling_101.html

Jenkins, H. (2011) Transmedia 202: Further Reflections. Accessed 20/3/15 at http://henryjenkins.org/2011/08/defining_transmedia_further_re.html

Jenkins, H. (2013) Transmedia Storytelling and Entertainment: A New Syllabus. Accessed 12/8/15 at http://henryjenkins.org/2013/08/transmedia-storytelling-and-entertainment-a-new-syllabus.html

Johnson, D. (2007) Fan-tagonism: Factions, Institutions, and Constitutive Hegemonies of Fandom. In *Fandom: Identities and Communities in a Mediated World*, eds. J. Gray, C. Sandvoss and C.L. Harrington. New York: New York University Press, 285–300.

Jones, M. (2011) Transmedia Storytelling Is Bullshit . . . . Accessed 20/3/15 at http://www.mikejones.tv/journal/2011/4/4/transmedia-storytelling-is-bullshit.html

Jones, M. (2012) Transmedia. It's Not a Brand. It's Not a Campaign. It's Not Fucking Advertising! Accessed 20/3/15 at http://www.mikejones.tv/journal/2012/7/9/transmedia-its-not-a-brand-its-not-a-campaign-its-not-fuckin.html

Joyce, M. (2001) *Othermindedness: The Emergence of Network Culture*. Ann Arbor: University of Michigan Press.

Nelles, W. (2012) Microfiction: What Makes a Very Short Story Very Short. *Narrative*, 20(1), 87–104.

Page, R., Harper, R. and Frobenius, M. (2013) From Small Stories to Networked Narrative: The Evolution of Personal Narratives in Facebook Status Updates. *Narrative Inquiry*, 23(1), 192–213.

Page, R. and Thomas, B. (2012) *New Narratives: Stories and Storytelling in the Digital Age.* Lincoln: University of Nebraska Press.

Pugh, S. (2005) *The Democratic Genre: Fan Fiction in a Literary Context.* Bridgend: Seren Books.

Ryan, M-L. (2001) *Narrative as Virtual Reality: Immersion and Interactivity in Literature and Electronic Media.* Baltimore: Johns Hopkins University Press.

Ryan, M-L. (2002) Beyond Myth and Metaphor: Narrative in Digital Media. *Poetics Today*, 23(4), 581–609.

Ryan, M-L. (2006) *Avatars of Story.* Minneapolis: University of Minnesota Press.

Ryan, M-L. (2013) Transmedial Storytelling and Transfictionality. *Poetics Today*, 34(3), 361–88.

Ryan, M-L. and Thon, J.N. (2014) *Storyworlds across Media: Towards a Media-Conscious Narratology.* Lincoln: University of Nebraska Press.

Sconce, J. (2004) Star Trek, Heaven's Gate, and Textual Transcendence. In *Cult Television*, eds. S. Gwenllian-Jones and R. Pearson. Minneapolis: University of Minnesota Press, 199–222.

Turk, T. (2011) Metalepsis in Fan Vids and Fan Fiction. In *Metalepsis in Popular Culture*, eds. K. Kukkonen and S. Klimek. Berlin: Walter de Gruyter, 83–103.

Walker, J. (2004) Distributed Narrative: Telling Stories Across Networks. In Paper presented at AOIR 5.0, Brighton UK. Accessed 20/3/15 at: http://jilltxt.net/txt/Walker-AoIR-3500words.pdf

Wolf, M.J.P. (2012) *Building Imaginary Worlds: The Theory and History of Subcreation.* London: Routledge.

9

CONCLUSION

'Narrative has remained ever present, ever up to date.'

(Altman 2008: 1)

As demonstrated in the preceding chapter, these are exciting times both for storytellers and for those interested in exploring how narrative works. In terms of our object of study, it is becoming increasingly difficult to talk of narrative texts as discrete entities, as storyworlds are now almost routinely delivered and encountered across a range of media and platforms. At the same time, the power of storytelling in its most traditional sense is recognised as never before, informing political campaigns, corporate communication as well as the entertainment and cultural industries the world over. One of the best examples of this is 'Brand Obama', combining some of the traditional tools of political rhetoric with contemporary marketing techniques, but relying heavily on autobiographical storytelling to connect the then–presidential candidate's own personal journey with that of the nation he was campaigning to lead (Lilleker 2014). Whether we celebrate or are sceptical of this 'storytelling revival' (Salmon 2010: 3), it is claimed that new uses are being found for narrative encompassing politics, journalism and the workplace.

As far as the study of narrative is concerned, technological advances have made it possible to analyse narratives in new ways, exploring recurring patterns or themes across vast datasets or using geolocation technologies to map how narratives are experienced, shared and spread across continents. But alongside these 'big data' approaches, researchers are finding that encouraging people to tell their own stories their own way may provide an effective alternative to cold, hard facts or quantities of information. In my own institution, researchers in health and social science have used storytelling techniques to explore attitudes of young mothers towards breastfeeding, the experiences of caregivers and those suffering from dementia and the personal histories of older lesbian and gay men. Stories here replace the more traditional methodologies of the questionnaire or the interview, but storytelling may also be a way of presenting findings, as in the case of the film *Rufus Stone* which turned the stories collected as part of the project 'Gay and Pleasant Land?' into a gripping drama about the experiences of a young boy discovering his sexuality in rural England (Jones and Hearing 2014).

Meanwhile, postclassical narratology continues to expand the focus of analysis beyond the literary text, particularly to engage with music, radio or the phenomenon of audiobooks as in the emerging field of 'audionarratology'. Much more attention is being paid by narrative researchers to readers and audiences, and to the affective and emotional responses narratives elicit, while cognitive narratology has raised the question of whether stories can help us better understand the mind, and how the mind may be affected by conditions such as autism or dementia. Whether or not we as humans are unique in our ability to generate endless stories may increasingly be brought into question as more sophisticated computer programs are devised, and as new fields of study open up new understandings of human–animal and trans-species relationships (e.g. Herman 2014). One of the most fundamental questions that may emerge from these developments is whether or not we need to look beyond language and examine how gesture, movement, kinetic and haptic dimensions contribute to the narrative experience.

Despite the pace and scale of change, the basics of narrative may be said to have remained a constant. Technological pyrotechnics may hold our interest temporarily, but it is compelling characters and plots that stimulate engagement and that sustain participation. Telling stories as an embodied 'live' activity continues to exert a fascination and to produce affective, powerful responses in audiences whether this is via story 'slams' or experiences recorded for YouTube or Vine. While some may complain that today many of these stories are manufactured and homogenised, there is also plenty of evidence to suggest that users and audiences continue to find ways to tell their stories in ways which can surprise and subvert expectations and accepted practices.

TO BE CONTINUED . . .

While we all enjoy a good ending, the best stories are perhaps those that continue to engage and stimulate us long after the show has ended or the book has been put away. In this introduction to narrative, I hope to have stimulated your interest in contemporary forms of narrative and how they may both reflect and shape some of our shared human experiences. This introduction to the basics of narrative should equip you to carry out your own analyses of examples across media, as well as pointing you to reading that will allow you to develop your analytical skills and explore examples in more depth. Maybe nothing beats a good story, but understanding how that story has been constructed and how we as audiences and readers respond and engage can be very rewarding. One thing is sure, we will never run out of new stories and new ways of telling stories to talk about and discuss, but perhaps we are only just beginning to fully recognise the role we play in bringing those stories to life and passing them on for others to enjoy.

REFERENCES

Altman, R. (2008) *A Theory of Narrative*. New York: Columbia University Press.

Herman, D. (2014) Narratology Beyond the Human. *Diegesis*. 3.2. Accessed 12/8/15 at https://www.diegesis.uni-wuppertal.de/index.php/diegesis/article/view/165

Jones, K. and Hearing, T. (2013) Turning Research into Film. In *Qualitative Research for the Social Sciences*, ed. M. Lichtman. London: Sage, 184–9.

Lilleker, D. (2014) Autobiography and Political Marketing: Narrative and the Obama Brand. In *Real Lives, Celebrity Stories: Narratives of Ordinary and Extraordinary People Across Media*, eds. B. Thomas and J. Round. London: Bloomsbury, 129–49.

Salmon, C. (2010) *Storytelling: Bewitching the Modern Mind*. Transl. D. Macey. London: Verso.

GLOSSARY

Binary Oppositions: In structuralist linguistics, meaning is said to derive from difference. Extending this idea to cultural formations and to narrative, binary oppositions structure our way of seeing the world as made up of fundamental tensions or conflicts, for example, good/evil, rich/poor, young/old. Narratives often revolve around these fundamental conflicts, but also play on the contradictions and tensions that exist within and between these oppositions.

Cognitive Narratology: Drawing on concepts and terminology from cognitive science and theory of mind, this approach focuses on the cognitive processes involved in reading narrative texts, as well as how those texts depict certain states of mind or habits of thinking.

Convergence: In relation to contemporary media and culture, as described by Jenkins (2006), an ongoing process whereby 'old' and 'new' media combine and collide. In a convergence culture, content continually flows between media and audiences actively participate by seeking out content and making connections across media.

Diegesis: Traditionally, diegesis and mimesis are used to refer to the distinction between 'telling' and 'showing'. In relation to tv and film narratives, diegesis refers to the particular world depicted in a narrative. Diegetic music can be heard by the characters, whereas nondiegetic music helps convey a certain atmosphere or mood to the audience but is not audible to those inhabiting the world of the narrative.

Distributed Narratives: Walker's (2004) theory of a kind of narrative made possible by the advent of the World Wide Web and network culture. Distributed narratives are fragmented and spread across time and space, with no single author or controlling figure.

Duration: Genette's (1980) theory concerning the speed of a narrative or how long a narrative takes to report an event. The account may take roughly the same amount of time as the event would take in reality. Alternatively, the reader is offered only a brief summary or the narrative stretches out a particular action or happening, as in the case of slow motion sequences in film.

Embedded Narratives: Stories within stories, for example, where a fictional character recounts a particular event. In a tv show this might occur where the contestants or participants relate their experiences of going on a date, taking part in a challenge etc. Narrative theorists have used metaphors of nesting, the layers of the onion, Russian dolls and stacking to try to explain this phenomenon.

Event: A fundamental unit of the action of the narrative (i.e. what drives it along). Sometimes defined as a change of state.

Extradiegetic Narration: Where the narrative is recounted from a position outside or 'above' the storyworld.

First Person Narration: A narrative told by an 'I' narrator, often but not always a character who takes part in the story and experiences the events being recounted (e.g. 'I was born in Wales but left to travel the world').

Flashback: Flashback, or analepsis, refers to the insertion into a narrative of events that happened chronologically earlier, for example, a character on her deathbed revisiting scenes from her childhood.

Flashforward: Also referred to as prolepsis, where events that haven't yet happened appear in the narrative, as in a premonition or foretelling of some kind of disaster.

Focalization: A narratological term introduced as an alternative to 'point of view'. According to Genette (1980), the focalizer is the entity who 'sees' in a narrative.

Frame: How the events of a narrative are shaped and bounded. For example, 'Once upon time' frames the beginning of a fairy tale, whereas 'They lived happily ever after' signals the end.

Free Indirect Discourse: Mainly used to refer to instances where a third person narrator represents in the course of his or her narrative the thoughts or uses the expressions of a character. Sometimes described as where the narrative is 'coloured' by the perspective of another, the device has been linked closely to the rise of the novel but is not confined to this form of narrative.

Frequency: Another term introduced by Genette (1980), in relation to how often events are recounted in a narrative. The norm is that we are told once about something that happened once, but it may be that we are told once about something that happened repeatedly, or that we are told repeatedly about an event that happened just once. As with duration, analysing frequency may provide an indication of an event's importance.

Gaps/Gap-Filling: No narrative can give an exhaustive account of every single thing that happens, and so we as readers or audiences draw on our imaginative resources to fill these gaps, drawing on our experiences, generic conventions and so on. The study of gaps and gap-filling has mainly focused on serial forms where, it is argued, gap-filling is an intrinsic part of the reader or viewer's pleasure in the text.

Gender: As opposed to sex, which is based on physiological differences between males and females, gender refers to the ways in which masculinity and femininity are socially constructed.

Genre: A type or kind of narrative. Attempts to categorise genre may refer to certain formal characteristics of the narrative or to the kind of experience it offers the viewer or reader.

Grand Narratives: Term used by Lyotard (1984) to refer to certain kinds of validating or legitimating discourses (religion, history, science) that offer us a view of the world in which the consequences of our actions appear inevitable and part of some kind of larger logic.

Heterodiegetic Narrator: A narrator who does not participate in the events he or she recounts.

Homodiegetic Narrator: A narrator who participates in events, typically one of the characters.

Hyperreality: The notion that in postmodern culture the distinction between an object and its representation has crumbled, so that we can no longer tell the difference between reality and its simulation.

Hypertext Fiction: A form of 'electronic fiction' that emerged during the 1980s where hypertextual links offer the reader different ways of navigating the texts, resulting in complex nonlinear narratives that are unrepeatable.

Ideology: Beliefs and norms that appear natural and obvious but which reflect the interests of the dominant class.

Implied Reader: As outlined by Iser (1974), not the actual reader or an ideal reader, but the reader that we assume to be the intended recipient from certain textual cues.

Intertextuality: The idea that every text contains echoes of and engages in dialogue with other texts.

Intradiegetic Narration: The narrative is recounted from within, for example, one character telling his or her story to another.

Lexia: A term introduced by Barthes (1975) now widely used in discussion of interactive or hypertext fiction to refer to nodes or blocks of text connected together by hyperlinks.

Ludology: The study of games, often positioning itself in opposition to narrative-based theories.

Metalepsis: In Genette's (1980) use of the term, a disruption of narrative levels or from outside the narrative.

Modernism: An artistic and literary movement from the early decades of the twentieth century which set out to challenge how human experience, memory and so on could be represented.

Myth: A narrative that through repeated telling comes to have particular force and significance for a cultural group or community. In Barthes's usage, the term is very close in meaning to ideology.

Narratee: The narrator's intended audience, particularly where the narrator explicitly addresses individuals or groups who are named and embodied.

Nowness: Fiske's (1987) term for a specific quality of tv narratives, offering audiences the real or perceived experience of sharing events with the characters or personages onscreen as they unfold.

Order: Genette's (1980) term for when events are recounted in a narrative. The telling of a story does not have to recount events chronologically, but can involve devices such as the flashback and the flashforward.

Paratext: A term originally coined by Genette (1997[1987]) to refer to material that acts as a threshold to the main narrative. As used by Jonathan Gray (2010), the term has been applied to contemporary media forms, to argue that marketing materials and seemingly peripheral material may contribute significantly to a film, videogame, or tv show's meaning.

Participatory Narrative: A narrative form (usually online) which relies on the participation of users. This participation may take a variety of forms, but reflects the principles and practices of a participatory culture as defined by Henry Jenkins (2006).

Postclassical Narratology: An umbrella term, covering the many ways in which contemporary theorists have responded to and reappraised classical narratological models and terms, including feminist and queer narratology, cognitive narratology etc.

Postmodernism: A cultural phase and literary and artistic movement from the sixties onwards. Postmodern narratives are often highly self-conscious and play with narrative form, especially nonlinearity.

Reception Theory: An umbrella term, sometimes used interchangeably with reader-response and audience theory, covering approaches which focus on the experience or process of reading, watching or listening to a narrative.

Second Person Narrative: A narrative told in the second person (e.g. 'You were born in Wales, but you travelled the world'). The form has recently received a lot of attention in relation to digital interactive fiction and unnatural narration.

Semiotics: The science and study of signs and sign systems. Particularly influential in the study of film and advertising.

Serial/Serialisation: Serial narratives are told in instalments and often feature multiple characters and plotlines which are developed and extended over long periods of time.

Structuralism: A view of the world in which we can only access and experience reality as it is structured for us by language or other cultural systems of meaning. Closely related to semiotics, in relation to narrative the term refers to the body of work produced by predominantly European philosophers and theorists in the 1960s, including Todorov, Lévi-Strauss and Barthes, concerned with exposing the underlying structures of narrative.

Text: Narratives seem to come to us in the form of some kind of bounded object or physical thing, for example a book, videogame, podcast etc. Barthes (1977) used the term 'text' in opposition to 'work' to move away from the notion of fixed material products, to explore ways in which the more fluid text continually responds to and interconnects with other texts as in the term intertexuality.

Third Person Narrative: A narrative told in the third person (e.g. 'She was born in Wales but left to travel the world'). Usually associated with narratives where the narrator is detached from the characters he or she tells us about, and often linked with omniscient narration, where the narrator appears to know everything about the events and characters he or she is relating.

Transmedia Storytelling: A term introduced by Henry Jenkins (2007) to refer to a narrative that is distributed and experienced across multiple media platforms. Attempts to define the practice have proved controversial. Competing terms used by narratologists include intermedial and transmedial narrative.

Unnatural Narration: A narrative which challenges or breaches our notion of what is 'natural' by contravening the laws of physics, logic etc. Examples might include narratives where characters seem to have impossible powers or stories that jump between time or geographical zones in ways that defy plausibility.

Unreliable Narrator: A narrator whose version of events cannot be trusted. This could be because of a deliberate desire to deceive his or her audience. However, the unreliability may also because of some lack of knowledge or insight that is unavoidable (e.g. a narrator who is too young to understand the full significance of the events he or she is recounting).

Worldbuilding: The construction of imaginary worlds within and across media, involving the active engagement of audiences.

WEB RESOURCES

Living Handbook of Narratology (Wiki/Open Access Resource)
http://www.lhn.uni-hamburg.de

Narrative Wiki (hosted by the International Society for the Study
of Narrative) http://narrative.georgetown.edu/wiki/index.php/
Main_Page

Semiotics for Beginners http://visual-memory.co.uk/daniel/
Documents/S4B/semiotic.html

A Guide to Narratological Film Analysis (Manfred Jahn) http://
www.uni-koeln.de/~ame02/pppf.htm

Gender Ads Project – resource of over 4000 ads http://www.
genderads.com

INDEX